D0292288

THE FORCE BORN OF TRUTH

MOHANDAS GANDHI
AND THE SALT MARCH,
India, 1930

BETSY **KUHN**

TFCB TWENTY-FIRST CENTURY BOOKS ■ MINNEAPOLIS

This book is dedicated to the work of all who are inspired by Gandhi.

Twenty-First Century Books
A division of Lerner Publishing Group, Inc.
241 First Avenue North
Minneapolis, MN 55401 U.S.A.

Website address: www.lernerbooks.com

Library of Congress Cataloging-in-Publication Data

Kuhn, Betsy.
    The force born of truth : Mohandas Gandhi and the Salt March, India, 1930 / by Betsy Kuhn.
        p.   cm. — (Civil rights struggles around the world)
    Includes bibliographical references and index.
    ISBN 978–0–8225–8968–6 (lib. bdg. : alk. paper)
    1. Gandhi, Mahatma, 1869–1948—Juvenile literature. 2. Gandhi, Mahatma, 1869–1948—Political and social views—Juvenile literature. 3. Salt—Political aspects—India—History—20th century—Juvenile literature. 4. Protest movements—India—History—20th century—Juvenile literature. 5. Civil rights movements—India—History—20th century—Juvenile literature. 6. Nonviolence—India—History—20th century—Juvenile literature. 7. India—History—Autonomy and independence movements—Juvenile literature. 8. India—Politics and government—1919–1947—Juvenile literature. 9. Nationalists—India—Biography—Juvenile literature. 10. Statesmen—India—Biography—Juvenile literature. I. Title.
DS481.G3K75 2011
954.03'5092—dc22 [B]   2009049127

Manufactured in the United States of America
1 – CG – 7/15/10

CONTENTS

DANDI, INDIA

The remote coastal village of Dandi in western India was usually quiet. Most days it seemed almost deserted. Yet, as the sun rose on the morning of April 6, 1930, Dandi teemed with thousands of people. They milled around on the black sandy beach beyond the village. Nearly everyone was dressed in white— white homespun clothes and little white caps—and they all seemed expectant. Something was about to happen here, something they could not bear to miss.

At 6:30 A.M., a small man dressed in a white loincloth approached the water. He was Mohandas Gandhi, a man so revered in India that the people called him Mahatma, or "Great Soul." For three weeks, he had been marching the dusty roads of India with seventy-eight followers. Gandhi and his compatriots had walked 241 miles (388 kilometers) to reach this tiny village on the Arabian Sea.

At nearly every stop along the way, hundreds of people had come to hear Gandhi speak. Much of what he had to say concerned the British. For as long as anyone alive at the time could remember, the British had ruled India. They had drained India's people of their spirit, their resources, and their very culture. Many felt that it was time for the British to leave and let Indians govern India.

But how were the Indians to drive out the British? The British Empire was vast and powerful. The British ruled so many countries around the world that it was said that the sun never set on the British Empire. British India was known as the Raj. That means "reign" or "rule" in Hindi, a major language in India. India was said to be the jewel in the crown of the empire, the most valuable of all Great Britain's possessions. The British government would not readily give up India.

All the same, Gandhi asked Indians to imagine a future independent of the British. He knew how Indians could begin to achieve this goal: they could make salt.

With miles of coastal salt flats and numerous salt mines, India had enough salt to supply the world. But the British had a monopoly on (total control of) India's salt. Under this monopoly, Indians were not allowed to produce their own salt. They could not so much as pick up a lump of rock salt or harvest it from the sea. Only the British could manufacture salt. The British had also imposed a tax on the purchase of salt. Since no one could live without salt, everyone in India, no matter how poor, paid the salt tax.

Gandhi said the salt laws were wrong. And British rule in India was wrong. On the beach at Dandi, Gandhi did what he had walked so far to do. Reaching down, he scooped up a handful of muddy sand and salt. He held it up and said, "With this salt, I am rocking the foundations of an Empire."

With that one simple gesture, Gandhi broke the British salt laws and started a revolution. When Gandhi raised his fist full of salt that day on Dandi beach, it was the beginning of the end of British rule in India.

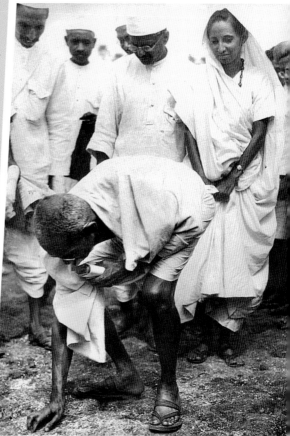

Mohandas Gandhi broke British law by picking up a lump of natural salt in Dandi, India, on April 6, 1930. This photo is a later reenactment of the historic moment.

CHAPTER 1

YOUNG
GANDHI

"Truth is what the voice
within tells you."

—Mohandas Gandhi, n.d.

Mohandas Karamchand Gandhi was born on October 2, 1869, in Porbandar, a town in the state of Gujarat, India. Although he would grow up to be one of the most influential people in history, Gandhi himself was quick to point out that he was not an exceptional child. He was a mediocre student, shy, and easily scared. "To be at school at the stroke of the hour and to run back home as soon as the school closed—that was my daily habit," he remembered. "I literally ran back, because I could not bear to talk to anybody."

Mohandas was the youngest child of Karamchand Gandhi, the local prime minister. His mother, Putlibai, was deeply religious. "She would not think of taking her meals without her daily prayers," Gandhi remembered. She visited the local Hindu temple every day, and she fasted regularly.

Gandhi's family practiced the Hindu religion, but he was exposed to other religions as well. Muslims and Hindus lived side by side in Porbandar. His father's friends included Muslims, Sikhs, and Parsis. They would visit the Gandhi home and discuss their faiths. Mohandas listened and gained respect and tolerance for all religions. Yet he felt no strong religious calling for himself.

In school Mohandas had trouble with multiplication tables and he said he had no

Gandhi was seven years old when this photo was taken in 1876.

talent for sports. Cricket and soccer were popular, but he played them only when he had to in school. He preferred long walks.

He also had a desire to always be truthful. Once, when Mohandas was in high school, the educational inspector paid a visit to his class. He gave the students five words to spell. Gandhi's teacher noticed that the young man had misspelled *kettle*. By nudging Mohandas with his boot, he urged him to copy from a classmate's slate. Mohandas would not. "The result was that all the boys, except myself, were found to have spelt every word correctly," he later wrote.

Mohandas was just thirteen years old when he was wed to Kasturbai, also thirteen, in an arranged marriage. He enjoyed the fuss and excitement of the wedding. Being married was a bit more bewildering. He and Kasturbai were initially shy with each other, but as they came to know each other, they talked easily. "I used to keep her awake till late in the night with my idle talk," wrote Gandhi.

He was determined to be a faithful husband. In turn, he expected equal dedication from Kasturbai. He insisted his young wife seek his permission before going anywhere. But "Kasturbai was not the girl

Gandhi and Kasturbai were married as teenagers in 1883. It was typical in India at this time for parents to arrange marriages for their children. This photograph was taken many years later.

to brook [put up with] any such thing," he wrote. "She made it a point to go out whenever and wherever she liked."

> **Gandhi was "a dashing cricketer" [cricket player] ... good at batting and bowling [pitching]."**
> —*Ratilal Ghelabhai Mehta, a high school classmate, 1958*

■ ■ ■ ■ THE BRITISH RAJ

When Gandhi was a boy, India was home to nearly 300 million people. They included a staggering mix of religions, castes, and ethnicities. The majority of the people were Hindu. Hindus lived according to a rigid caste system in which a person's place in society was determined from birth. The highest caste was the Brahmans, traditionally reserved for priests. Gandhi's family belonged to the Bania, or merchant, caste. The lowest group in Hindu society was the untouchables. Untouchables, in modern times called Dalits, were deemed to be so unworthy that they existed outside of the caste system.

India was also home to Muslims, as well as Parsis, Buddhists, Jains, Sikhs, and Christians. The various peoples of India spoke more than one hundred different languages. The upper classes learned English in school.

The British ruled directly over only part of India. The rest of the country was broken up into hundreds of princely states. Each of these states was under the control of a local ruler who had pledged his loyalty to the British in exchange for military protection. Either directly or indirectly, through the local princes, the British ruled all of India.

Britons had first arrived in India as traders with the British East India Company in the early 1600s. Over the next century, the British vied with Portuguese, Dutch, and French trading companies for power in this vast, resource-rich country. By the late 1700s, the British East India Company controlled virtually all of India.

The majority of Indians are Hindu, but the population also includes
Buddhists, Christians, Jains, Muslims, Parsis, and Sikhs.

Buddhists

Buddhism was founded in present-day Nepal by Siddhartha Gautama
(the Buddha), who lived in the sixth century B.C. Buddhists do not
believe in a god or gods, but seek spiritual growth by meditating on
Four Noble Truths: (1) life is full of suffering; (2) desire is the cause of
suffering; (3) suffering can be ended by ending desire; and (4) desire
can be stopped by following the Middle Way, that is, being neither too
self-indulgent nor too self-denying. Buddhists believe in reincarnation,
or rebirth, on the path to nirvana, a state of complete joy with
compassion for all.

Christians

Christians practice Christianity, a monotheistic (one god) religion based
on the teachings of Jesus Christ, whom Christians believe to be the
son of God. Their holy text is the Bible, including the New Testament,
which details Christ's life and lessons for mankind. Christians believe
in following the teachings of Jesus, in loving God and one another, and
that Jesus died so that humanity's sins could be forgiven.

Hindus

The Hindu religion dates back thousands of years. Hindus believe in
one Supreme God as well as the existence of other gods. Their religion
is based on karma, the principle of cause and effect, whereby a person's
karma—good and bad actions—affects what happens to that person
later in life. Hindus also believe that a person's soul is reincarnated
many times on the path to enlightenment, or moksha, the liberation
from the cycle of rebirth. Because of the Hindu practice of ahimsa
(nonviolence), Hindus traditionally have been vegetarian.

Jains

The overriding principle of Jainism, an ancient religion of India, is ahimsa: nonviolence in thought and deed. Jains—followers of Jainism—believe that all living things, including insects, should be treated with respect. For this reason, Jains are vegetarians. Jains believe in reincarnation and living a life of self-denial as a way of achieving enlightenment.

Muslims

Muslims follow the religion of Islam, a word that means "submission to the will of God." Muslims believe in one God, Allah, and that his most important prophet was Mohammed, who was born in the city of Mecca, in Saudi Arabia, in A.D. 571. Among other things, Muslims practice the Five Pillars of Islam, which include praying five times a day and making a pilgrimage, if possible, during one's lifetime to Mecca. The spiritual text of Islam is the Quran.

Parsis

Parsis are descendants of Iranian Zoroastrians, who came to India from Iran (then known as Persia) more than one thousand years ago. The majority of them settled in the Indian state of Gujarat. Zoroastrianism was founded around 1200 B.C. in the Middle East by the prophet Zoroaster. Zoroastrians believe in one god, Ahura Mazda. They see life on Earth as a battle between good and evil. Parsis strive for good by following the Zoroastrian ideals of good thoughts, good words, and good deeds. Sacred fires, which symbolize the light of Ahura Mazda, play a central role in Zoroastrian ceremonies.

Sikhs

The Sikh religion was founded in India by Guru Nanak, born in 1469. Sikhs believe in one god, whom each person must strive to understand by studying the world he created and by looking for him within themselves. Like Hindus, Sikhs believe in karma and a cycle of rebirth as the soul journeys toward an enlightened, liberated state. The Sikh holy scripture is called the Sri Guru Granth Sahib (Book of God).

The East India Company's dominance in India created tension with the local peoples over issues such as the company's unfair trading practices and racism. In 1857 the tension erupted in a massive rebellion, known as the Indian Rebellion of 1857, or the Sepoy Rebellion. Angry sepoys (Indian soldiers serving under British command) murdered British officers and slaughtered entire British families.

The British government responded by taking control of India from the East India Company in 1858. This meant the British government in faraway London, England, made all the decisions about India, including its economy and foreign affairs. Great Britain built railroads and bridges in India. It established a civil service, a system of government agencies to oversee everyday needs of citizens. Indians were hired for many of these jobs, but the British controlled the civil service, the court system, and the military.

British troops and Indian rebels clash during the Siege of Delhi in 1857. The siege was a major battle in the Indian Rebellion.

■ THE COLONIAL ECONOMY

One of the main reasons for building an empire is to gain new markets in which to sell a country's goods. For the British, salt was one of these goods. In 1670 the British discovered an immense deposit of rock salt in Cheshire, England. To create buyers for all that salt, the British government soon imposed a salt monopoly in India. India had always had plenty of salt of its own. It had never had to import a grain of this vital commodity. But under the British monopoly, the people of India were no longer allowed to make their own salt. They had to buy British salt or salt manufactured by the British in India. The British also imposed a tax on salt. The salt tax touched every Indian, rich or poor.

THE **GREAT HEDGE**

Orissa Province on the Bay of Bengal in eastern India was home to some of the country's best salt deposits. But the ample supply of Orissa salt hurt sales of British salt. To protect the British salt industry, in 1804 the British claimed a monopoly on Orissa salt. Only they could manufacture, sell, or transport salt in Orissa. They imposed a heavy tax on all salt sales.

For a while, the salt makers in Orissa survived by selling salt illegally in the neighboring province of Bengal. The British were determined to stop the salt smuggling. In the 1840s, they began to construct a massive hedge along the border of the two provinces. It was a living wall of thorns and dense vegetation 14 feet (4.25 meters) high and 12 feet (3.6 m) thick. At its completion, it was 2,500 miles (4,023 km) long (more than the distance between Chicago, Illinois, and Portland, Oregon), and twelve thousand people patrolled its length. In the twenty-first century, only traces of the Great Hedge remain.

1498   Vasco da Gama, a Portuguese explorer, discovers a sea route from Europe to the East Indies (present-day Indonesia and nearby islands) by sailing around the Cape of Good Hope, the southern tip of Africa. His discovery sets off a frantic race among European traders to establish trading centers in the East.

1600   England's Queen Elizabeth I grants a charter (legal contract) to the East India Company, which gives the company exclusive rights to trade on England's behalf in Asia.

1608   East India Company traders reach India, but the Portuguese are already there and send the English away.

1616   The East India Company secures the right to establish a trading center in Surat, India.

1696   The East India Company establishes Fort William in Calcutta (present-day Kolkata), India. The company operates three major trading centers—Madras (Chennai), Bombay (Mumbai), and Calcutta (Kolkata).

1697   The thriving East India Company is the largest employer in London. The company imports Indian textiles such as calicos, silks, and muslins. The textiles prove so popular in England that its linen and woolen businesses suffer. Parliament (Great Britain's lawmaking body) passes laws restricting imports of Indian cottons.

1773 The East India Company faces financial difficulties. The British government provides an enormous loan to the company in exchange for partial control.

Mid-1700s through mid-1850s Through a series of wars and battles with local rulers, the East India Company becomes the dominant governing power in India.

1857 The Sepoy Rebellion erupts. A rumor circulates among sepoys, Indian soldiers serving under the British, that company officials are going to force them to convert to Christianity. Another rumor reports that the British are introducing ammunition cartridges greased with pork or beef fat. To use the cartridges, the sepoys will have to bite them open. The pork would violate Islamic dietary law, and the beef would violate Hindu dietary law. The Hindu and Muslim sepoys stage a violent rebellion. They murder British officers and families.

1858 After the Sepoy Rebellion, Queen Victoria of Great Britain proclaims, "We have resolved . . . to take upon ourselves the government of the territories in India." The proclamation concludes that the gratitude of the people of India will be "our best reward." The highest British official in India will be a viceroy, a representative of the queen. Native princes are allowed to keep authority over their states as long as they vow loyalty to the British.

British rule also devastated the Indian textile industry. India had once been the leading cotton textile producer in the world. Hand spinning and hand weaving provided a living for vast numbers of Indians. When the British began trading with India in the 1600s and 1700s, Indian cottons became a wildly popular import in Great Britain. At one point, English wool merchants demanded that Parliament limit imports of Indian cottons. English buyers were choosing Indian cotton over British wool, hurting the wool merchants' business.

Then came the Industrial Revolution of the 1800s. New inventions and new machinery brought methods of mass production, which began to replace manual labor and cottage (home-based) industries. In

FROM INDIA TO BOSTON HARBOR

Troubles in the East India Company had a direct effect on the history of colonial North America. In 1773 the British government extended a massive loan to the East India Company to save it from bankruptcy. To pay back the loan, the company gave the British government warehouses full of Chinese tea. The British decided to sell the tea to the colonists in North America who were under British rule. However, the British had imposed a tax on tea that was highly unpopular with the colonists. Three ships loaded with tea reached Boston Harbor (in Massachusetts) in early winter 1773. To protest the tea tax, on December 16, colonial patriots (who favored independence) dressed as Mohawk Indians boarded the ships, split open the wooden crates of tea, and dumped their contents into Boston Harbor. This event is known as the Boston Tea Party and was one of the events leading to the American War of Independence (1775–1783).

Great Britain, huge textile mills began producing massive amounts of cloth. Industrial leaders needed markets in which to sell the cloth. They argued that, instead of importing Indian cloth, Great Britain should be exporting its textiles to India and other markets. For these reasons, cheap British cloth flooded the Indian market. Indians began wearing cloth from Great Britain instead of cotton made in India, and the Indian textile industry dwindled.

A TERRIBLE DECEPTION

Young Mohandas Gandhi had little interaction with the British. Still, he shared the general resentment felt by most Indians. When he was a teenager, this young man who was so devoted to truth committed a terrible deception, largely because of the British. He had befriended another Hindu boy who secretly ate meat. The Hindu religion forbids meat eating, but the friend rationalized his action. Meat, the friend told Gandhi, was what made the British strong.

Gandhi began to think about eating meat to get stronger, like the British. Although his parents had raised him to avoid meat, Gandhi began to believe his friend. The friend was daring and athletic. Gandhi was relatively weak. Plus, "I was a coward," he wrote. "It was almost impossible for me to sleep in the dark, as I would imagine ghosts coming from one direction, thieves from another and serpents from a third." His own wife, he knew, had more courage than he did. Gandhi did not want to be a coward. He wanted to be strong and fearless— and not just for his own sake. He thought that perhaps, "if the whole country took to meat-eating, the English could be overcome."

Driven by that thought, Gandhi began to eat meat secretly. His first attempt, eating goat meat, made him sick and gave him nightmares. "Every time I dropped off to sleep it would seem as though a live goat were bleating inside me." Eventually he learned to tolerate meat. Yet he could not tolerate deceiving his parents.

Finally, Gandhi realized, that "deceiving and lying to one's father and mother is worse than not eating meat." He stopped eating meat and never ate it again. But he did not give up his dream of overcoming the British.

The people of India did not organize politically against British oppression until the 1880s, when Lord Ripon became viceroy of India. Ripon, a reformer, supported the Ilbert Bill. It sought to bring equality to India's legal system. Although both British and Indian judges oversaw trials, a European could request to be tried before a British judge. Under the Ilbert Bill, Indian judges would be allowed to try and sentence Europeans. The bill, if passed, would put Europeans (most of whom were British) on equal legal footing with Indians. Indians welcomed the proposal. Not so the Europeans. The European outcry against the Ilbert Bill was loud, vicious, and racist. Imagine your wife, wrote one European opponent, being tried by "a copper-colored Pagan [non-Christian]."

Just as the Ilbert Bill united its opponents, it also united those who supported it. Until then, Indians who sought greater rights had defined themselves by their differences: different provincial backgrounds, castes, or religions. In fighting for the Ilbert Bill, those differences became unimportant. According to the Lahore Times, because of the Ilbert Bill, "a growing feeling of national unity which otherwise would have taken [Indians] years to form, suddenly developed into strong sentiments."

The Ilbert Bill never passed. Even so, it was the driving force behind the creation of the Indian National Congress (INC), which met for the first time in 1885. The INC originally sought a greater role in government for Indians. Eventually, it would become the most influential organization in the Indian independence movement.

■ OFF TO GREAT BRITAIN

In 1888, at the age of eighteen, Gandhi set forth on a new path. He went to Great Britain to study law. It was not unusual for prosperous Indian families to send their sons to Britain to be educated. Most of these young men returned to India to take jobs in the civil service or court system.

By this time, Gandhi's father had died. His mother agreed to let her son go abroad, but she worried about him. Great Britain abounded with Western temptations, and Gandhi would be far from the protective surroundings of home. Before allowing him to leave, she made him take a vow. He must promise to avoid meat, women, and wine. Gandhi took the vow. He left Kasturbai and a newborn son, Harilal, and sailed for England.

The hustle and bustle of London was vastly different from the Indian community where Gandhi had spent most of his life. London in 1888 was a sprawling metropolis of six million people. When Gandhi arrived that fall, the police were frantically searching for a brutal serial killer. Nicknamed Jack the Ripper, he had already killed a number of prostitutes in the slums of London's East End.

At first, Gandhi was homesick. He also was hungry a lot because he refused to eat the meat that made up so much of the British diet. And he disliked the way the British prepared vegetables—plain and boiled in contrast to India's spicy cuisine. Still as shy as ever, he hadn't the nerve to ask for something else.

As the months went by, Gandhi learned how to feed himself. He found vegetarian restaurants. Soon he was studying books about vegetarianism. The subject so fascinated him, in fact, that he organized a vegetarian society and met other vegetarians. His work with the vegetarian society marked his first try at organizing around a common cause.

Gandhi had more trouble figuring out how to behave in Great Britain. Initially, he felt he should try to become as British as possible. He bought new clothes, including a fancy hat. He signed up for dancing and elocution (public speaking) lessons. Before long he remembered that he was in England to become a lawyer, not to become an Englishman. One day he would be returning to India. Gandhi stopped the dancing and elocution lessons. He continued to wear his fine English clothing though.

Gandhi *(circled)* joined the Vegetarian Society in London. This picture shows the members of the society in 1890.

During his time in Britain, Gandhi learned to live simply, not only as a way of saving money but also to encourage his spiritual growth. He rented rooms that allowed him to walk to the places he needed to be. Walking 8 to 10 miles (10 to 16 km) a day, he wrote, "kept me practically free from illness throughout my stay in England and gave me a fairly strong body."

In Britain, Gandhi began reading newspapers for the first time. "In India, I had never read a newspaper," he wrote. In London he "always glanced over *The Daily News, The Daily Telegraph,* and *The Pall Mall Gazette.*"

Gandhi also became interested in religious texts. He read the Bhagavad Gita, a sacred Hindu text. He found it inspiring and continued to read it regularly. At a friend's urging, Gandhi read the Bible. The New Testament appealed to him, "especially the Sermon on the Mount which went straight to my heart," he wrote. In the Sermon on the Mount, Jesus presents lessons on living a holy life to his followers. "The verses, 'But I say unto you, that ye resist not evil: but whosoever shall smite thee on thy right cheek, turn to him the other also. And if any man take away thy coat let him have thy cloak too,' delighted me beyond measure," Gandhi wrote. This message of peace in response to violence became a key part of Gandhi's philosophy of nonviolent resistance to injustice.

When Gandhi completed his law studies, he gathered his friends for a farewell dinner. He planned to make a short speech. But still shy and uncomfortable speaking in public, he later wrote, "I could not proceed beyond the first sentence."

At his dinner, Gandhi managed only to thank his guests for joining him. He wondered if he would ever make another speech. He also worried whether he could succeed as a barrister (trial lawyer). He felt horribly unprepared. "I had serious misgivings as to whether I should be able even to earn a living by the [legal] profession," he wrote.

Although he was awash with doubts about his future, the young man passed his examinations, joined the High Court as a barrister (much as a lawyer is admitted to the bar in the United States) on June 11, 1891, and sailed for India the next day. He had but one ray of hope to guide him as he left England. An older, respected friend had promised him that, to be a successful lawyer, he needed only to be honest and hardworking. "And as I had a fair share of these last," wrote Gandhi, "I felt somewhat reassured."

CHAPTER 2

GANDHI
IN SOUTH AFRICA

"Nonviolence is the first article
of my faith. It is also the last
article of my creed."

—Mohandas Gandhi, March 18, 1922

When Gandhi arrived back in India, his brother met him at the dock in Bombay. Gandhi had barely stepped off the ship when his brother told him their mother had died. The news was a terrible blow. He took comfort in knowing that he had kept his vow to avoid wine, women, and meat.

Gandhi opened a law practice in Bombay, but his first court appearance was an embarrassment. When he had to cross-examine a witness, he later wrote, "My heart sank into my boots. I could think of no question to ask." He removed himself from the case, ashamed. In the meantime, his household and professional expenses were piling up. His family was growing too. In 1892 Kasturbai gave birth to another son, Manilal. "I felt a crushing sense of responsibility," Gandhi wrote.

Gandhi's fortunes began to change when he was asked to handle a case for a group of Indian businessmen in South Africa. The work would require him to spend about a year there. Gandhi accepted the offer.

ON THE MARITZBURG PLATFORM

In April 1893, Gandhi bid good-bye to Kasturbai and their two sons and set sail for South Africa. There, he arrived in the port city of Durban, in the British-held province of Natal. At the time, South Africa was a patchwork of British- and Dutch-controlled colonies. The British provinces primarily occupied the southern, coastal tip of South Africa. The Dutch provinces, which included the Transvaal and the Orange Free State, were located to the northeast of the British-held territory.

South Africa was home to a sizable Indian population. Beginning in the 1860s, European settlers had recruited Indians to come to South Africa as indentured servants to work in the sugarcane fields. Under the terms of their indenture, Indian laborers had to work for five years as virtual slaves. After five years, they were free to go back to India or settle in South Africa. Many Indians stayed on, and many established successful farms and businesses.

Durban is a bustling port city on the east coast of South Africa. This photograph was taken in 1902.

Success had not brought equality, however. Gandhi had been in Natal for less than a month when he had to travel to Pretoria, in the Dutch-held province of Transvaal, for his legal case. He booked a first-class train ticket and began his journey. That evening the train pulled into the station at Maritzburg (formally Pietermaritzburg), a mountain town in Natal. A railway official came to Gandhi's compartment. He stunned Gandhi by saying that he had to leave his first-class seat and move to third class.

Gandhi pointed out that he had a first-class ticket, but the official was unmoved. Because Gandhi was Indian, he would have to leave the compartment or the official would call a police constable. "The constable came," remembered Gandhi. "He took me by the hand and pushed me out." As Gandhi struggled to compose himself, the train chugged out of sight. It was winter in South Africa, and Maritzburg was freezing cold. Gandhi's overcoat was packed away with his luggage, which the railway personnel had locked in the station. Gandhi spent all night on the station platform, shivering and thinking.

"I began to think of my duty," he wrote. "Should I fight for my rights or go back to India, or should I go on to Pretoria?" He began to feel a new sense of courage and purpose. He was not turning back. He would continue on to Pretoria.

The humiliating journey was hardly over, though. The next day, when he boarded a stagecoach to Pretoria, the white coachman made him sit outside with the driver rather than share the coach with white passengers. Later, that same coachman commanded Gandhi to sit on the footboard and give the coachman his seat. When Gandhi refused, the coachman swore at Gandhi and beat him. The passengers inside the coach complained and insisted on bringing Gandhi inside.

When the coach stopped overnight in a village, Gandhi asked for a hotel room. The hotel manager took one look at him, saw he was Indian, and told him the hotel was full. Gandhi stayed that night with an Indian associate of his law firm. "This country is not for men like you," said Gandhi's new Indian friend. "First and second class tickets are never issued to Indians." It was just as impossible for an Indian to book a room in a hotel.

When Gandhi at last reached the city of Pretoria, he learned more about how poorly European colonists in South Africa treated Indians. Indians could not vote or own land except in certain areas. They could not walk on public footpaths or be out at night without a permit.

Gandhi could not understand how Indians in South Africa tolerated such unfair treatment. He invited every Indian in Pretoria to a meeting to discuss their situation. Gandhi, who had always been frightened of speaking in public, had no trouble addressing the group. He urged them to work together regardless of their differences, whether Hindu or Muslim, or from Gujarat or the Punjab in India. Only by setting aside their differences could they make their voices heard.

The group began to meet regularly. "I saw that South Africa was no country for a self-respecting Indian," wrote Gandhi, "and my mind became more and more occupied with the question as to how this state of things might be improved."

During Gandhi's time in South Africa, three books made lasting impressions on him: *The Kingdom of God Is Within You* (1894), by Russian author Leo Tolstoy; *On Civil Disobedience* (1849), by American Henry David Thoreau; and *Unto This Last* (1860), by Englishman John Ruskin.

In *The Kingdom of God Is Within You*, Tolstoy argued for combating evil with nonviolence, or passive resistance. Later, in 1908, Tolstoy wrote *Letter to a Hindu*, which maintained that the people of India could overcome British rule through love and nonviolence. After reading *Letter to a Hindu*, Gandhi began corresponding regularly with Tolstoy, refining and developing his philosophy of effecting change.

In July 1846, Henry David Thoreau spent a night in the Concord, Massachusetts, jail for refusing to pay his taxes. He was protesting the U.S. government's support of slavery and its participation in the Mexican-American War (1846–1848). Later, he explained his beliefs in an essay entitled *On Civil Disobedience*. "The only obligation which I have a right to assume is to do at any time what I think right," wrote Thoreau. He believed it is not enough to say a law is wrong. A person has to take action, that is, disobey wrong laws. Civil disobedience lies at the heart of Gandhi's philosophy.

John Ruskin's *Unto This Last* excited Gandhi with its philosophy that "the good of the individual is contained in the good of all," that all work has value, and that "a life of labour, the life of the tiller of the soil and the handicraftsman is the life worth living."

In Pretoria, Gandhi's skills as a lawyer grew as well. He ultimately was able to settle the case that he had come to South Africa to handle. He worked out an agreement between the opposing parties that satisfied everyone. "I realized that the true function of a lawyer was to unite parties riven asunder [split apart]," he wrote. From then on, he was a confident and highly skilled lawyer.

Gandhi was also growing spiritually. He read the Quran and other key books to understand the Islamic religion. He studied books about Christianity. One book, in particular, stood out. "Tolstoy's *The Kingdom of God Is Within You* overwhelmed me," wrote Gandhi. Leo Tolstoy, a Russian author of the nineteenth century, is best known for novels such as *Anna Karenina* and *War and Peace*. Late in life, Tolstoy wrote about spiritual matters. *The Kingdom of God Is Within You* picks up where Jesus's Sermon on the Mount left off. Tolstoy wrote that passive resistance—turning the other cheek—was a better path to change than violence. Love and moral strength would succeed where violence and war never could.

▪ ▪ ▪ GANDHI STAYS ON

Having settled the case that brought him to South Africa, Gandhi prepared to return to India. First he went back to Durban. His friends there hosted a farewell party for him. At the party, a newspaper article caught his eye. It discussed a new legislative bill that would restrict the voting rights of Indians in Natal. "This bill, if it passes into law, will make our lot extremely difficult," Gandhi told his friends. "It is the first nail in our coffin." One of the guests asked Gandhi to stay in Natal to fight the bill. He agreed on the spot. "The farewell party was thus turned into a working committee," he wrote.

Under Gandhi's leadership, the Natal Indian community, which included people of various religions, castes, and provincial backgrounds, organized against the voting bill. They drew up a petition, gathered ten thousand signatures, and submitted it to the British government in Durban. The petition argued that Indians, as citizens of the British Empire, had voting rights in India. Therefore, they should enjoy similar voting rights in the British province of Natal. Gandhi knew that it was not enough to appeal to the British government. He and his fellow Indians also needed to gain support by educating as many people as possible about the cause of Indian voting rights. He sent copies of the petition to "all the newspapers and publicists I knew."

In 1894, barely a year after that bitter cold night on the Maritzburg railway platform, Gandhi created the Natal Indian Congress (NIC). The congress aimed to protect the rights and improve the lives of Indians in Natal. Initially, the group attracted well-to-do Indians who could afford NIC membership fees. Gandhi wanted the NIC to speak for all Indians, though, not just the wealthy ones.

One day an indentured servant in ragged clothes came to Gandhi for legal help. His name was Balasundaram. His teeth were broken and his mouth was bleeding because his master had beaten him. Gandhi, taking up his case, arranged a transfer to a new master. The news of Balasundaram's case spread quickly among indentured servants. They realized they had someone who would speak for them. In this way, Gandhi was able to take up the struggle for still more Indians.

Gandhi *(back row center)* and the other co-founders of the Natal Indian Congress pose for a photo in 1895.

By now, Gandhi realized that he was going to be in South Africa for a long time. In 1896 he traveled to India to bring Kasturbai and their children back to Durban.

THE BOER WAR

In 1899 war broke out in South Africa between the Boers—the Dutch—and the British. Gandhi had spent the last four years challenging the British treatment of South African Indians in Natal. Still, he supported the British in the war, called the war. If Indians were demanding their rights as British citizens, he said, they should fight for the British. He organized an ambulance service, made up of more than one thousand Indians, including more than seven hundred indentured workers. They often worked under enemy fire to remove wounded soldiers from the battlefield.

The Indian ambulance service helped to bring the Indian community together. It also fostered goodwill between the British and the Indians. (The mother of one British soldier was so grateful to Gandhi that she sent him a pair of hand-knitted socks every year.) When the British won the war in 1900, Indians were optimistic that their situation in South Africa would soon improve. With their victory, the British gained control of the provinces formerly held by the Dutch, including the Transvaal. Many Indians were convinced the British would strike down oppressive laws after the Indians had been so loyal in the war.

In fact, the outlook for Indians in South Africa appeared so bright that in 1901 Gandhi returned to India with his family. For the first time, he attended the Indian National Congress. The INC had flourished since its founding in 1885. The group mainly pressed for greater political representation for the Indian people within British-controlled India. Congressional leaders had different opinions on how to gain political power, though. Gopal Krishna Gokhale was the leading congressional spokesperson for a moderate approach. Indians should seek freedom gradually, he said, maintaining a dialogue with the British. Another Congress leader, Bal Gangadhar Tilak, was not willing to be so patient. "Swaraj [self-rule that would come with complete independence] is my birthright, and I shall have it!" he insisted.

While Gandhi was in India, he spent time with Gokhale. Gandhi was impressed by Gokhale's political work, as well as his efforts to end poverty and improve education. Gokhale was as impressed by Gandhi and his work in South Africa. Over time, he would become one of Gandhi's most important mentors.

GANDHI AND **HIS CHILDREN**

Gandhi and Kasturbai had four sons. Harilal (1888–1948) and Manilal (1892–1956) were born in India. Ramdas (1897–1969) and Devdas (1900–1957) were born in South Africa. Gandhi could be very tough as a father. Just as he had high expectations of himself, he had similar expectations of his family members. His children became unwitting subjects of his experiments in living a simple, non-Western life. For instance, Gandhi chose to teach them at home because he felt that traditional schools were too closely aligned with a Western lifestyle. What's more, he felt that developing a good character was at least as important as pursuing traditional studies. With the help of Indian tutors, he not only taught his sons the standard academic subjects, but he insisted that they help on the farm and perform household tasks, including emptying chamber pots (small pots used as toilets).

Gandhi's demands and beliefs affected his children differently. Harilal, in particular, bristled under Gandhi's demands. When Gandhi refused to allow Harilal to attend law school in London, Harilal's resentment deepened. Ultimately, Harilal rejected his father. He became an alcoholic. He converted for a time to Islam.

The other sons struggled to varying degrees to meet their father's high expectations. As they grew older, all three participated in Gandhi's

THE BIRTH OF SATYAGRAHA

Just as Gandhi and his family were beginning to feel settled in India, his friends in Natal called upon him once again. Life had not improved under the British. Rather, it had become worse. In late 1902, Gandhi returned to South Africa. He set up a law office in Johannesburg, in Transvaal. At a friend's suggestion, he started a newspaper, *Indian Opinion*.

struggle for Indian independence and spent time in prison for their political resistance.

Two sons, Manilal and Devdas, became journalists. Manilal returned to South Africa in 1918 to assume the editorship of *Indian Opinion*, the influential newspaper Gandhi had started in 1903. In 1930 he returned to India to participate in the Salt March and the civil disobedience movement and was imprisoned. Afterward, he went back to South Africa, where he continued to edit *Indian Opinion* and work toward abolishing apartheid, the South African laws defining the relationship between whites and blacks, which kept black people subjugated. Devdas became an editor of the *Hindustan Times*, a major Indian newspaper launched in the early days of the Indian independence movement in India.

Kasturbai Gandhi poses with her four sons in South Africa in 1902.

Gandhi *(center)* and his coworkers pose in front of his law office in Johannesburg, South Africa, in the early 1900s.

Creating a newspaper was a natural next step for him. It was the perfect vehicle for publicizing the Indian point of view.

Gandhi soon began another new venture. On a long train ride in 1904, he read *Unto This Last*, by British writer John Ruskin. In the book, Ruskin argued for economic equality for all workers and warned against the industrial movement. After reading it, said Gandhi, "I could not get any sleep that night. I determined to change my life in accordance to the ideals of the book." He bought a large piece of land outside of Durban and established the Phoenix Settlement, where Indians could work the land and embrace simple living.

Gandhi's focus, however, continued to be Indian rights. In 1906 the Transvaal government proposed a new ordinance (law) to keep Indians from entering Transvaal illegally. The Transvaal Asiatic Ordinance would require that Indians register with the government, give their fingerprints, and carry permits, or face punishment. Gandhi, outraged, called a mass meeting. Three thousand Indians gathered in the Empire Theatre in Johannesburg. They pledged to disobey the ordinance even if it meant imprisonment.

Despite this opposition, the new Transvaal Parliament passed the ordinance in 1907. Gandhi and the Transvaal Indians discussed how to fight back. Gandhi considered passive resistance. It was a nonviolent approach to conflict, echoing the lesson from the Sermon on the Mount. If someone strikes you on the cheek, offer them the other one.

Gandhi lived in this house at the Phoenix Settlement outside of Durban, South Africa.

Gandhi was a man of action. He developed a new approach. He called it satyagraha, which means "soul force, or the force born of truth." Satyagraha is nonviolent action, led by a person's sense of moral truth.

Gandhi used satyagraha to challenge the new registration laws. In meetings and in Indian Opinion, he urged Transvaal Indians to refuse to register. Just as he'd expected, Gandhi wound up in jail, briefly, for the first time. Soon General Jan Christiaan Smuts, colonial secretary of the Transvaal, offered a compromise. If Indians registered voluntarily, the government would repeal the act. Gandhi agreed, called off satyagraha, and registered.

Just months later, however, government officials reneged on their agreement. They declared registration mandatory and made it illegal for an Indian to enter Transvaal without a registration certificate. Upon hearing this news, Gandhi promptly called for satyagraha to resume. That summer thousands of Indians who had registered voluntarily gathered to burn their registration cards.

Next, under Gandhi's lead, they took on the law that forbade Indians from entering Transvaal without registration certificates. Satyagraha called for nonviolent action, so Gandhi and other satyagrahis attempted to cross into Transvaal without the certificates. As a result, Gandhi was sentenced to three months in prison. So many satyagrahis deliberately crossed the border without registrations that, at one point, one-fifth of the Transvaal Indian population was in jail. Satyagraha continued for two years as the government repeatedly refused to repeal the law.

As Gandhi's influence grew, he realized he needed a place for his followers to gather. In 1910 he established Tolstoy Farm outside of Johannesburg. As at the Phoenix Settlement, Gandhi practiced simple living. He baked bread, slept out in the open, and learned how to make furniture and sandals. Tolstoy Farm served as a temporary home for the families of resisters who were in prison and a home base for them between prison sentences. Most important, Tolstoy Farm served as a training ground for satyagraha. "The mode of life accepted by the satyagrahis on the Farm became an invaluable asset in the struggle," Gandhi wrote. Because the resisters lived simply on the farm, they

Gandhi and some friends and family sit near a tent on the Tolstoy Farm outside of Johannesburg in 1910.

were better prepared for prison and other hardships they encountered during their resistance.

■ ■ ■ THE GREAT MARCH

In 1911 the South African states were reorganized as the Union of South Africa, under the leadership of Prime Minister Louis Botha and General Smuts. Their leadership brought no positive changes for Indians. The registration law remained, along with a law imposing a tax on indentured servants. Furthermore, a new court ruling decreed all non-Christian marriages illegal. As a result of this ruling, "The whole [Indian] community rose like a surging wave," wrote Gandhi.

While living in South Africa, Gandhi never stopped thinking about India. In 1908 he wrote a booklet, Hind Swaraj, which means "Indian home rule." The booklet addressed not only the issue of Indian independence from British colonial rule but also that of Indians and modern civilization. According to Hind Swaraj, it was not enough for the British to leave India. Indians had to also reject the British way of life to be truly free. "You want English rule without the Englishmen," Gandhi wrote. "You want the tiger's nature, but not the tiger; that is to say, you would make India English. And when it becomes English, it will be called not Hindustan but Englishtan. This is not the Swaraj I want."

Many Indian women joined the fight, incensed at the notion that their Hindu or Muslim marriages were invalid. Gandhi's supporters included men, women (including Gandhi's wife, Kasturbai), Hindus, Muslims, Christians, indentured servants, and wealthy traders. Under his leadership, they demanded a repeal of the tax, the marriage law, and the registration law. Then they unleashed the biggest satyagraha campaign yet.

The women started civil resistance by violating the illegal entry ban. One group of women marched from Transvaal into Natal without registrations cards, while another crossed from Natal into Transvaal. The women entering Transvaal were quickly arrested and imprisoned. The ones entering Natal, however, were undisturbed. They then proceeded to march to the coal mines of Newcastle, where they urged the indentured workers to protest the new laws by going on strike (refusing to work).

> **"I have read your book [*Hind Swaraj*] with great interest because I think the question you treat in it: the passive resistance—is a question of the greatest importance, not only for India but for the whole humanity."**
> —Leo Tolstoy to Gandhi, letter, May 8, 1910

At this point, the government arrested the women, but not in time to stop thousands of miners from dropping their tools and going on strike. Gandhi put these new supporters to use. On November 6, 1913, at 6:30 A.M., he set off with more than two thousand striking miners and their families on a march to Transvaal. They knew they faced arrest when they reached the border. If they were allowed to pass, they would continue their march to Tolstoy Farm.

Gandhi instructed the members of the Great March, as it became known, how to conduct themselves as satyagrahis. They were to submit willingly to arrest, endure beatings patiently, continue on if Gandhi were arrested, and conduct themselves in a clean and moral fashion.

Gandhi and the marchers crossed the border into Transvaal that first morning. During the first two days of the march, Gandhi was arrested twice and released. When officials arrested him a third time, approximately 80 miles (128 km) into the march, they held him. The marchers continued on until they reached the town of Balfour, nearly 100 miles (161 km) from where they set out. There, they were shipped back by train to the coal mines, where they found the owners had converted the mines into prisons. The miners were subjected to brutal treatment, and a number were killed. In response, more indentured servants went on strike. Thousands more Indians were in jail. South Africa was in turmoil.

The government, in response, released Gandhi from prison. As a show of solidarity with Indians, he had given up Western clothes. Instead of wearing suits, he wore Indian clothing: a kurta (a long, loose-fitting shirt), loose-fitting pants, and a turban.

On march through Volksrust.

Indians in South Africa march through the town of Volksrust in the Transvaal on November 6, 1913, to protest laws limiting Indian freedom.

■ WORLD RECOGNITION

Gandhi's clothes had changed, but his goals were the same. He announced another mass march to begin on New Year's Day, 1914. At this news, railway workers decided to go on strike in support. The government imposed martial law, using military force to control its citizens.

The South African situation had become so heated that newspapers worldwide covered the story. It was then that Gandhi appears to have received his first mention in the *New York Times.* "From the government's standpoint," said an article of January 14, 1914, "about the only ray of light to-day was the assurance of the Indian leader, Gandhi, that the passive resistance movement by the Indians against their grievances would be dropped during the present trouble."

Gandhi called off the mass march in light of the railway strike. He did not want to challenge the government at such a turbulent time. He felt it went against the principles of satyagraha—treating one's opponent fairly and changing their opinion through thoughtful moral persuasion.

General Smuts and Gandhi had been facing off for years, and Smuts had learned to respect Gandhi and his methods. They negotiated an agreement, the Smuts-Gandhi Pact, and this time, Smuts stood by his word. The pact of June 30, 1914, repealed the tax on indentured servants, recognized non-Christian marriages, stopped the Indian indentured servant system as of 1920, and changed the laws regarding Indian movement into and around South Africa.

Soon after, Gandhi and his family left South Africa. The young man who had arrived in 1893 so full of doubt about his future was forty-four years old. Far from being a tongue-tied new barrister, he had found his voice. Moreover, he was returning to India with a powerful new weapon for change: satyagraha.

CHAPTER 3

GANDHI RETURNS TO INDIA

"We said what we felt and shouted it out from the housetops. What did we care for the consequences? Prison? We looked forward to it."

—Jawaharlal Nehru, INC president and future prime minister of India recalling the events of 1921, 1941

■ ■ ■ ■ **Before returning to their beloved India, Gandhi and Kasturbai sailed first for Britain.** Gandhi hoped to meet with British leaders to advance the Indian cause of independence. This project would have to wait, though. During the course of his journey, the Great War—also known as World War I (1914–1918)—began. As Gandhi's ship entered the English Channel separating France and England, it had to slow down to pick its way past submarine mines. They had been laid to protect the Channel from enemy German submarines.

Wartime was no time to make demands for Indians, Gandhi decided. Rather, he felt, Indians should be helping the British war effort. If Indians wanted the full rights of British citizens, he argued, then they must behave as British citizens during the war.

At that time, a well-known Indian poet named Sarojini Naidu lived in London. Naidu was active in Indian politics and a close friend of Gokhale. She was also helping to make clothes and bandages for the wounded soldiers. Gokhale suggested that she enlist Gandhi's aid, so she went to visit Gandhi and Kasturbai in their small London apartment.

Naidu recalled climbing "the steep stairs of an old, unfashionable house, to find an open door." Inside she saw a small, virtually bald man, sitting on the floor. He was "eating a messy meal of squashed tomatoes and olive oil out of a wooden prison bowl," she noted. So this was the great Indian leader! "I burst instinctively into happy laughter," she wrote. Gandhi

Sarojini Naidu, shown here in the 1920s, was an Indian poet active in Indian politics. She became a friend of Gandhi in London during World War I.

laughed right back. "Ah, you must be Mrs. Naidu!" he said. "Who else dare be so irreverent?" Then he asked her to share his meal.

"No, thanks," she replied. "What an abominable mess it is!" They both laughed again. So began a great friendship between Naidu and Gandhi. Politically they had a lot in common. In terms of personality, though, they were like night and day. Where Gandhi embraced simple living, simple food, and simple clothes, Naidu embraced all the vibrancy, good food, and color that life offered. She would light up a room with her brightly colored saris (women's wrap of silk or cotton fabric) of orange and peacock blue.

That fall in London, she spent a lot of time with the Gandhis. "Men of all nations—Eastern and Western—gathered in his home," she remembered, drawn by Gandhi's powerful message. Naidu admired Kasturbai as well, "a kindly, gentle lady, with the indomitable spirit of the martyr."

DOMINION STATUS

In 1914, when Gandhi left South Africa, Great Britain was the largest empire on Earth. King George V, who had ascended the throne in 1910, reigned over 11 million square miles (18 million square km) of territory around the globe and more than 400 million people. Yet, the countries that made up the empire were not equals. The British government had granted dominion status, that is, home rule, to Canada, Australia, New Zealand, Newfoundland, and the Union of South Africa. All were governed by white men. Countries such as India, in which the native population sought home rule, continued to operate under British control.

The Gandhis returned to India in January 1915. Gandhi's work in South Africa had made him internationally known, and Indians welcomed him back to India as a hero. Rabindranath Tagore, one of the country's most revered poets and winner of the 1913 Nobel Prize in Literature, bestowed on Gandhi his nickname: Mahatma (Great Soul).

For all the excitement over Gandhi's arrival, however, Gokhale was adamant that Gandhi take time to know his country again. He had been mostly gone for more than twenty years, and he hadn't really known India all that well before leaving for South Africa. Gandhi promised that he would spend a year not speaking publicly but listening and watching.

Gandhi (dressed in white with a dark hat) is welcomed back to India in 1915. He is sitting in the cab of the carriage.

Gokhale's advice was some of the last that he would give Gandhi. In February 1915, Gokhale died. The great moderate leader of Indian nationalism (promoting India as an independent country) and the champion of Indian education was gone.

Gandhi kept his promise to Gokhale. For seven months, he traveled the length and breadth of India. He rode third class on trains and made every effort to see his country as the poorest Indians saw it. What he saw was a country populated by mostly very impoverished people trying to eke out a living from the land. According to the 1911 census, 72 percent of Indians were involved in some form of agriculture, from farming the land to raising livestock. Approximately 285 million Indians lived in rural areas, while only 29 million made their homes in urban centers. More than 200 million Indians were

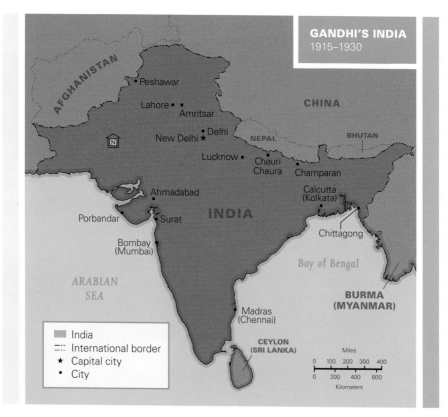

Hindu, the country's dominant religion. Sixty-six million Indians were Muslim, while the rest were mostly Sikhs, Buddhists, Christians, and other religions.

The majority of the Indian population could not read or write. While the census found that fewer than 17 million Indian men were literate, close to 144 million were illiterate. The difference was even more pronounced among women. Just 1.6 million women were found to be literate. More than 151 million were illiterate. Indian males were far more likely to attend school of any kind—from primary school through university—than females.

Throughout his tour of India, Gandhi was repeatedly distressed by the lack of sanitation. Not only did he find that many Indians failed to maintain any kind of personal cleanliness, he found a general lack of sanitation in villages, cities, and public transport. He described making a boat trip as a deck passenger (akin to third class). The bathroom "was unbearably dirty, the latrines were stinking sinks. To use the latrine one had to wade through urine and excreta [solid waste] or jump over them." The passengers "spat where they sat, dirtied the surroundings with the leavings of their food, tobacco and betel leaves." Gandhi determined to educate his fellow Indians on basic sanitation and cleanliness.

BRINGING BACK THE SPINNING WHEEL

Gandhi was eager to establish a place in India similar to Tolstoy Farm, where he could put his beliefs about simple living and satyagraha to work. He established the Sabarmati Ashram (spiritual community) outside of Ahmadabad, in the province of Gujarat. He chose this location for several reasons. For one thing, he had grown up in Gujarat. He felt at home there, and the people of Gujarat made him feel welcome. What's more, the ashram site was close to the local jail. Gandhi knew from his experiences in South Africa that satyagrahis could expect to spend time behind bars.

Finally, he chose the location because, as he pointed out, the city of Ahmadabad was "the ancient center of handloom weaving." Spinning and weaving had once played a vital role in the Indian economy. Under British rule, these cottage industries had died out as imported British textiles flooded Indian markets. At the time of Gandhi's return in 1915, most Indians wore fabrics made in Great Britain. Meanwhile, millions of impoverished Indians had no way of making a living.

Gandhi believed that reintroducing spinning and weaving as cottage industries would help to ease poverty in India and make the people self-reliant again. By establishing his ashram in an area once known for handloom weaving, he figured that the making of *khadi* (homespun cloth) would flourish there.

It was easy enough to establish practices of simple living at the ashram. The people who lived at the ashram, the ashramites, strove to be self-sufficient. Everyone participated in the work of farming, tending the orchards, cooking, and cleaning. Unlike the rest of India, no caste system was allowed within the walls of the ashram. The ashramites performed for themselves the tasks that in the rest of India an untouchable would do, such as cleaning toilets. Women at the ashram were treated as equals by men, another break from tradition.

Setting up the ashram as a spinning and weaving center proved to be challenging. Gandhi had started writing about the benefits of hand spinning while in South Africa. Yet by 1915, he had never actually seen a spinning wheel. When he set up the ashram, the ashramites brought in some hand looms. "But no sooner had we done this," Gandhi wrote, "than we found ourselves up against a difficulty." Not one of them knew how to use them! A weaver was brought in. Eventually members of the ashram learned how to weave.

When it came to spinning yarn, the challenge was more daunting. Try as they might, Gandhi and the other ashramites could find no one who knew how to spin. What once had been a core cottage industry was, as Gandhi said, "all but exterminated." After much searching, Gandhi at last found spinners to train members of the ashram.

"The wheel began merrily to hum in my room," Gandhi remembered, as he took up spinning. It was not long afterward that he began wearing a dhoti (wrapped fabric shorts) made of hand-spun cloth. From then on, Gandhi spent part of every day spinning.

Gandhi spins thread at an ashram in the 1930s. Gandhi believed that spinning and weaving were key to Indian self-reliance.

THE LUCKNOW PACT

Heeding Gokhale's advice, Gandhi stayed out of politics until he became reacquainted with his country. He remained silent during a particularly dynamic time in Indian politics. For many years, the country's various factions had clashed. Hindus and Muslims, for instance, had long distrusted one another. In 1906 Muslims had created the All-India Muslim League to make sure their voices were heard in the predominantly Hindu country. The members of the Indian National Congress itself were divided among the moderates, who argued that home rule should come gradually, and those who were eager to run the British out of the country and assume home rule as soon as possible.

In 1916 members of the Indian National Congress and the All-India Muslim League set aside their religious differences for the greater good of independence. Both groups held their annual meetings that December in the city of Lucknow in northern India. In a rare stroke of unity, they drew up the Lucknow Pact. Through the work of Muslim leader Mohammed Ali Jinnah, the pact promised Muslims ample representation alongside Hindus in a new independent government. The pact was such a milestone that Sarojini Naidu, who was also in Lucknow, was swept up by the vision of a free and unified India. She called Jinnah the Ambassador of Hindu-Muslim Unity.

Gandhi was in Lucknow that December too, but he continued to stay on the sidelines. Silence from such a renowned leader puzzled many of the attendees. According to young activist Jawaharlal Nehru, who was twenty-seven at the time, Gandhi "seemed very distant and different and unpolitical to many of us young men. . . . He refused to take part in Congress or national politics and confined himself to the South African question."

Nehru, no doubt, had hoped to see Gandhi more outspoken. He certainly was hungry for such a leader. A son of Motilal Nehru, a prominent moderate leader, Jawaharlal Nehru was burning to see a more dynamic independence movement. He had no patience for moderates, like his father, who seemed willing to plod dutifully along, accepting British platitudes about greater self-governance. "I felt that both individual and national honor demanded a more aggressive and fighting attitude toward home rule," Nehru wrote.

Above: Mohammed Ali Jinnah was a leader in the Muslim movement for India's independence. *Right:* Jawaharlal Nehru was a Hindu leader who also worked for Indian independence.

GANDHI RETURNS TO PUBLIC LIFE

After the Lucknow conference, a poor peasant named Rajkumar Shukla drew Gandhi back to public life. Shukla pleaded with Gandhi to come to Champaran, his village, to help the tenant farmers. Greedy plantation owners were forcing the farmers to pay higher rents and mandating what they could grow. The farmers were left starving and destitute.

Gandhi agreed to visit Champaran, a village at the base of the Himalayas in the northeastern province of Bihar. The plantation owners tried to force him out of town, but Gandhi politely refused to leave. He stayed in Champaran for most of 1917 and gathered thousands of statements from tenant farmers about their troubles. As a result, the Bihar government appointed a committee to investigate the tenant farmers' plight. The committee ultimately passed a law in favor of the tenant farmers. Under the new law, the plantation owners could not impose rent increases. They even had to refund much of the money they had collected from the tenant farmers. In addition, Gandhi arranged for a doctor to provide the peasants much needed medical care. Kasturbai joined him in Champaran and, with the help of doctors, introduced

A group of Indian cavalry rides through Marseille, France, during World War I.

sound sanitation practices. They worked with the villagers to clear the village of filth and educate them on personal cleanliness. Gandhi, the nonviolent activist, had returned to public life.

Gandhi's "victory in Champaran ... filled us with enthusiasm," said Nehru. "We saw that he was prepared to apply his methods in India and they promised success."

Meanwhile, the Great War was still raging. More than one million Indians were fighting for the British Empire. Indians raised millions of dollars for the war and supplied huge amounts of wheat and rice to feed British troops and civilians as well.

POSTWAR ACTIONS

When the war ended on November 11, 1918, with a British victory, the people of India were hopeful. They had given much to the war effort, and they thought perhaps, in gratitude, the British would grant India dominion status. Dominion status would mean that the country, though still a member of the British Empire, would be self-governing. Canada, Australia, New Zealand, Newfoundland, and the Union of South Africa had dominion status within the empire. In 1917 Edwin S. Montagu, the secretary of state for India, had announced a policy that seemed to imply that India would gradually gain dominion status as well.

India's once-great textile industry had suffered greatly under the British Raj. From 1917 to 1918, India imported more than six hundred times more manufactured cotton from the United Kingdom than it exported to the United Kingdom.

Things worked out differently, however. Perhaps knowing that the Indian people expected more independence after the war, the British actually tightened the reins. During the war, the British had imposed certain restrictions on civil liberties. They had imprisoned a number of nationalist leaders under oppressive wartime laws. With the war over, they moved to make the laws permanent. In March 1919, Great Britain passed the Rowlatt Acts. Under these acts, the government could imprison political suspects without a trial and try political prisoners without a jury.

Gandhi, like many Indians, felt duped and insulted. The acts, he felt, were "altogether unwarranted" and that "no self-respecting people could submit to them." One night Gandhi fell asleep thinking about the Rowlatt Acts. "I was still in that twilight condition between sleep and consciousness when suddenly the idea broke upon me." The next morning, he announced his plan. The people of India would stage a one-day general *hartal*, or strike. For that one day, they would stay home from work and school, close their businesses, and spend the day in fasting and prayer.

The hartal was held on April 6, 1919. Stores, banks, schools—everything—simply shut down. In some cities, the strike gave way to violence, including rioting and arson. When Gandhi learned of the violence, he realized he had moved too quickly. He needed time to educate the people of India about the methods of satyagraha. He fasted for three days as penance for the outbreaks.

THE AMRITSAR MASSACRE

In the city of Amritsar, in the Punjab, discontent continued to simmer. When officials arrested two local government leaders, the people of Amritsar crowded the streets in protest. The demonstrations led to rioting, and the violence got out of hand. Five Britons were killed, and a British missionary woman was assaulted. Such news would have spurred any government official to action. The British official in charge of Amritsar, Brigadier General Reginald Dyer, saw fit to take drastic steps—with tragic results. On April 12, 1919, he issued an order prohibiting public gatherings, but it is unclear whether the people of Amritsar knew about the order.

Amritsar is in north central India. This photograph from 1919 shows one of its most famous sites, the Golden Temple.

On April 13, thousands of Indians gathered in Jallianwalla Bagh, a large courtyard in Amritsar. The courtyard was entirely surrounded by tall buildings. It was only accessible by one long, narrow street. The meeting was to be a peaceful protest against British repression and the violence committed by their own people.

When General Dyer learned of the gathering, he was determined to crush it. He led fifty soldiers through the narrow street that fed into the courtyard. He had also brought machine guns mounted on armored cars, but they could not pass through the narrow street. Then, without giving the people gathered in the courtyard the slightest warning, he ordered his men to open fire.

"The soldiers fired 1,600 rounds in ten minutes and nearly every bullet found its mark," wrote author William Shirer. In ten minutes, they killed 379 men, women, and children and wounded 1,137 more. Because the courtyard was enclosed, there was no means of escape. British soldiers blocked the only way out. A number of people tried to duck the guns by jumping into an old well, and they drowned.

Later, Dyer testified that he had ordered his men to fire into places where the crowd was thickest. By showing the people of Amritsar that the British meant business, "I thought I would be doing a jolly lot of good," he testified.

But General Dyer wasn't finished. He still felt compelled to extract his revenge for the assault on the British missionary woman, and he issued a "crawling order." Whenever an Indian traveled the British woman's street, he or she had to crawl down it, "like worms on their bellies," noted Gandhi. To be sure the crawling order was followed, Dyer stationed soldiers, armed with bayonets, along the street.

No mention of the Amritsar massacre appeared in U.S. newspapers such as the *New York Times* or the *Washington Post* until December of that year. That month the British government conducted an official inquiry into the incident. As the inquiry proceeded, the United States and the rest of the world began to learn what had happened.

At the time of the investigation, Jawaharlal Nehru was traveling on a night train from Amritsar to Delhi. From his curtained sleeping booth, he heard a military officer speaking in "an aggressive and triumphant tone," wrote Nehru. He boasted "how he had the whole town at his mercy and he had felt like reducing the rebellious city to a heap of ashes, but he took pity on it and refrained." The officer turned out to be Dyer.

■■■■ NONCOOPERATION

The massacre at Amritsar and the crawling order severed all loyalty Gandhi had felt to the British. In 1920 he called for a lengthy campaign of noncooperation. Indians, he urged, should simply refuse to cooperate with any British institution. Students should quit attending British

Jallianwalla Bagh, the site of the Amritsar Massacre in 1919, has been preserved as a park. A plaque commemorates those who died in the massacre. The well where people drowned trying to escape the bullets is there, as are some of the walls, still riddled with bullet holes.

schools. Lawyers should refuse to appear in British courts. He urged Indians to boycott British goods, including the endless shipments of textiles from Great Britain's mills. If the Indian people kept up the noncooperation movement, Gandhi maintained, the British would grant India independence in a year.

Gandhi had become a major force in India, a full-fledged national leader at the very center of India's nationalist movement. The Indian National Congress looked to him for direction. Millions of Indians revered him. They affectionately called him Bapu, the Hindi word for "father." At his urging, noncooperation swept the country. Gandhi traveled the country for months, speaking to gatherings that often numbered one hundred thousand people or more. He set bonfires, burning heaps of British-made textiles. He encouraged his fellow Indians to take up the spinning wheel as he had done and become self-sufficient. All along, he preached Hindu-Muslim unity.

"We were full of excitement and optimism and a buoyant enthusiasm. . . . The old feeling of oppression and frustration was completely gone."
—Jawaharlal Nehru, in reference to the campaign of noncooperation, 1920

Gandhi was not the only person ever to lead a boycott against imported British textiles. In the days leading up to the Revolutionary War, American colonists boycotted imported British cloth, too. Colonists sponsored spinning schools and held spinning bees to create their own homespun. In 1769, for instance, the women of Lancaster, Pennsylvania, produced 35,000 yards (32,000 m) of homespun. In 1768 and 1769, Harvard and Yale universities voted to allow graduating seniors to wear homespun suits to commencement so "that none . . . may be obliged to the hard necessity of unfashionable singularity [looking odd] by wearing imported cloth."

Even Motilal Nehru, a lifelong moderate, joined the noncooperation movement. Some national leaders, however, such as Mohammed Ali Jinnah of the Muslim League, disapproved of it. As a result, Muslim-Hindu unity began to splinter.

Gandhi was also back in the newspaper business. He became editor for the weekly English-language newspaper, *Young India*, and a weekly Gujarati paper, *Navajivan*. He filled the pages with articles about noncooperation, blasting the British government for the crimes it had committed against India. "Non-cooperation," he wrote in no uncertain terms, "deliberately aims at the overthrow of the government."

Throughout 1921 more than ten thousand activists, including Jawaharlal Nehru and other congressional members, were arrested for political actions and jailed. "There seemed to be an inexhaustible supply of volunteers for prison," Nehru wrote. They were eager to go to jail in the name of the independence movement.

Followers of Gandhi burn non-Indian cloth in the streets of Delhi in 1922.

CHAURI CHAURA

Gandhi had made it clear that the noncooperation movement was to be nonviolent. Nevertheless, some Indians resorted to violence. Early in 1922, in the town of Chauri Chaura, police officers tangled with a group of protesters. The protesters chased the officers, who ran into the city hall for safety. The mob set fire to the hall. When the twenty-two officers ran out to escape the blaze, the mob viciously attacked and killed them. Gandhi was horrified. Without hesitation, he called off civil disobedience. Independence was not to be won by bloodshed, he insisted.

While many Indians supported his decision, others, like Nehru, did not. "We were angry when we learned of this stoppage of our struggle at a time when we seemed to be . . . advancing on all fronts," he wrote. But he and so many others were in prison and unable to act. "Civil resistance stopped, and noncooperation wilted away."

On March 10, 1922, the British arrested Gandhi for sedition (planning to overthrow the government), citing his articles in *Young India*. They tried him in Ahmadabad on March 18 before Judge C. N. Broomfield. As Kasturbai and Sarojini Naidu sat among the onlookers, Gandhi pleaded guilty to the charges.

He went on to explain at length to the court how he had lost faith in British rule. He presented a summary of the ways the British had drained India culturally, politically, and economically. The laws in India, he said, were created to benefit the British and exploit the Indians. Worse still, he said, the British—and the Indians who cooperated with them—did not even realize they were doing anything wrong. "The greater misfortune is that the Englishmen and their Indian

The deaths at Chauri Chaura *(below)* in 1922 horrified Gandhi and led him to call off civil disobedience.

associates in the administration of the country do not know that they are engaged in the crime I have attempted to describe." When Gandhi finished speaking, Judge Broomfield said, "I hate to have to do this," and sentenced Gandhi to six years in prison.

"This was not the last time the British arrested and imprisoned Gandhi," wrote Louis Fischer in his biography of Gandhi. "But it was the last time they tried him."

CHAPTER 4

SETTING THE **STAGE**

> You sit in your little room and spin: but the long, long thoughts you think as you twist the long, long thread reach out aross the world."
>
> —Sarojini Naidu, poet, in a letter to Gandhi, July 20, 1926

After Gandhi's trial in 1922, the feverish activity of the prior year died out. Gandhi went off to prison, and the independence movement lost much of its momentum. Indians who had marched resolutely out of schools and government jobs returned to them. Indian lawyers returned to the British courts. Worse, the unity that Muslims and Hindus had forged in 1916 at Lucknow had mostly dissolved.

The government released Gandhi from prison after two years when he suffered a bout of appendicitis. He did not consider his prison term over, however. The judge had given him six years' confinement, so he chose to stay out of the spotlight until 1928.

THE SIMON COMMISSION

Meanwhile, changes that would affect India were under way in the British Parliament. Conservatives had dominated British politics for most of the decade. In 1927 the Labour (liberal) Party appeared to be on the verge of sweeping the Conservatives out of office. Conservatives worried that reform-minded Labour leaders would grant India greater self-rule. So before Labour came into power, Conservative politicians created the Simon Commission to study the Indian government and recommend reforms. The commission was made up entirely of white British politicians. Not one Indian was among them to argue the Indian point of view.

The appointment of the Simon Commission lit a fire under the independence movement. Indians were furious that the British would so pointedly keep them out of deciding their country's future. When members of the commission arrived in India in early February 1928, Indians greeted them with black flags as a symbol of disapproval. They launched boycotts of British-run businesses and staged demonstrations. In the midst of one demonstration, police killed a popular local leader with a *lathi* (a long bamboo staff tipped with iron or steel). His death only stoked the Indian cause. More people turned out for later protests.

When the members of the Simon Commission arrived in

Lucknow, Jawaharlal Nehru was among the thousands of demonstrators. As the crowd marched through the city, he noted, "We saw in the far distance a moving mass. It was two or three long lines of cavalry or mounted police . . . galloping down toward us." Moments later, the horsemen were upon the marchers. "We held our ground," said Nehru. The horses, pulling up, "reared up on their hind legs with their front hoofs quivering in the air over our heads." The police began beating the demonstrators with lathis and batons. "It was a tremendous hammering," said Nehru. "All I knew was that I had to stay where I was and must not yield or go back." Eventually, the beating subsided while, noted Nehru, "the cause of all this trouble, the Simon Commission, secretly crept away from the station . . . more than half a mile [1 km] away."

That summer India's nationalist leaders responded to the Simon Commission by gathering representatives of the major Indian political parties. Under the leadership of Motilal Nehru, they drafted what became known as the Nehru Report. The report spelled out a constitution for India as a dominion in the British Empire. Gandhi was among the report's many supporters.

India's Muslim leaders, however, found the Nehru Report unacceptable. Under the proposed government, Muslims would lose the exceptions granted them under the Lucknow Pact. The government proposed by the Nehru Report would leave Muslims outside the ruling powers. The Hindu and Muslim rift widened.

THE "DRAIN INSPECTOR'S REPORT"

That same year, India took another harsh blow, this time in the form of a book. A U.S. writer, Katherine Mayo, published *Mother India*. In it she painted a picture of India as squalid, impoverished, and nearly inhuman. "Compared with millions of homes in India at this moment," said a reviewer in the *New York Times*, "Uncle Tom's Cabin [the slave shack in Harriet Beecher Stowe's famous 1852 novel, *Uncle Tom's Cabin*] must have been a paradise of liberty, sanitation, and culture." What's more, according to Mayo, the blame for these conditions lay squarely with the Indians. "India's distresses are India's fault," she wrote. "If she [India] has an enemy, it is the Mahatma," that is, Gandhi.

The book sold a quarter of a million copies worldwide. In India, however, the book stirred a massive outcry. "It has whipped Hindu India into a frenzy," noted the *New York Times*. "The pages of the Indian press bristle with denunciations of the book."

Gandhi, for his part, likened the book to "a drain inspector's report." Certainly, Mayo had uncovered some unsavory truths about India, he admitted, just as a drain inspector would in his work. But she reported them as if they captured India as a whole. Just as a drain offers but one narrow view of a home, Mayo had failed to provide a full and fair picture of India. Clearly, an Indian representative of exceptional intelligence, good humor, and charm needed to tour the United States to counter the book's damage. Who better to do so than Sarojini Naidu?

In the fall of 1928, representing Gandhi and the Indian National

Congress, Naidu sailed to the United States. When she stepped off the ship in New York, reporters asked her what she thought of Katherine Mayo. "Who is she?" Naidu retorted with characteristic spirit.

Naidu's tour took her throughout the United States and Canada, from New York City to California. She loved Arizona and the Grand Canyon. In her brightly colored saris, she spoke to groups nationwide, presenting India's story. "Like the founders of your Republic," she said in one speech, "the Young India of today has proclaimed to the world a Declaration of Independence." She called Gandhi, whom Mayo had attacked in her book, "spiritually the greatest living symbol of our age."

Naidu visited the Dana Hall School in Wellesley, Massachusetts, where she spoke to the five hundred female students, ages ten to

NAIDU IN THE UNITED STATES

Sarojini Naidu wrote to Gandhi in February 1929: "California I loved, every flowering... and foam kissed acre of that lovely land. But one sorrow made a cloud for me in that horizon of dazzling sunshine—the unhappy plight of the Indian settlers who after twenty or thirty years of prosperous labours on their own farm lands have by the recent immigration laws been deprived of all right to land and citizenship. They are reduced to working, most of them, as day labourers on the soil of which they were not so long ago masters."

Naidu is referring to a U.S. immigration ruling by the U.S. Supreme Court that denied people from India the right to become naturalized citizens. In 1923 the Court ruled in U.S. v. Bhagat Singh Thind that naturalized citizenship was reserved only for European whites. It was not until the 1940s that the U.S. Congress gave Indians the right to become naturalized citizens.

twenty. After the talk, headmistress Dorothy Waldo wrote to Gandhi, thrilled by the visit. Since Naidu's presentation, Waldo wrote, "I have heard girl after girl say, 'Gandhi seems real to me now and I know what he is trying to do.'"

When Naidu sailed back to India in the summer of 1929, Gandhi wrote that she had "returned none too soon to take her share in solving the many and intricate problems facing us in the country." The independence movement had had a most eventful year, and the nationalists would need all hands on deck in the year to come.

■ ■ ■ AN ULTIMATUM

In December 1928, while Naidu was in the United States, the Indian National Congress held its annual meeting in Calcutta. That year the outrage over the Simon Commission and *Mother India* had brought the independence movement roaring back to life. Nationalist leaders were ready to take a major step forward. In Calcutta they passed a bold resolution. If the British did not grant India dominion status in a year's time—by December 31, 1929—then INC Congress would declare swaraj. After it declared complete independence, it would then launch a massive campaign of nonviolent noncooperation.

With this ultimatum as a starting point, the year 1929 unfolded. Gandhi was busy lighting bonfires from heaps of British cloth. Congressional committees led campaigns against drinking and drugs. Strikes and demonstrations flared up around the country, and Indian newspapers ran nationalist articles promoting independence.

The British, for their part, responded to these new campaigns by conducting massive searches of activists' homes. They banned anti-British books and shut down activist newspapers.

Even so, nationalists had reason to be hopeful. That May, as predicted, the Labour Party came into power. The new prime minister was Ramsay MacDonald, a pacifist (person against wars) who had once hobnobbed with some of India's most progressive thinkers. Many pro-independence citizens hoped his government would be sympathetic to the nationalist cause.

The viceroy in India at this time was Lord Irwin. That summer Lord Irwin sailed to Great Britain to discuss the situation in India. In October he returned with what he called a "momentous statement." He proposed a round table conference where representatives from India and Great Britain could discuss India's political future for attaining dominion status.

Never before had a British official used the word dominion when discussing India's future. While many congressional members embraced the idea, others, such as Jawaharlal Nehru, did not. Nehru's group wanted nothing short of complete independence. Dominion status seemed a lukewarm alternative. Congressional members followed up on Irwin's proposal. Despite internal disagreement, they announced that they supported a round table conference but only if it involved an India with full dominion status.

In London Lord Irwin's suggestion of dominion status had created a furor. Parliamentary leaders were outraged at such a notion. They brought such pressure to bear on Irwin that all talk of dominion status ceased.

December arrived. The British had come no closer to granting India dominion status. If they failed to do so by December 31 (the deadline set forth by the Indian National Congress), India would declare independence in the form of massive civil disobedience. Time was running out.

Over Christmas the Indian National Congress held their annual meeting in Lahore. A nominating committee had asked Gandhi to serve as INC president. He declined. The right person for the job, he said, was Jawaharlal Nehru.

On the night of December 31, 1929, as the clock struck midnight, it was Nehru, then, who unfurled an immense, tricolor independence flag. "A happy new year and an era of independence," he shouted as crowds cheered.

The wheels had been set in motion for swaraj. When the signal was given, the people of India would engage in a mass civil disobedience campaign. What form this campaign would take was up to one man: Gandhi.

■ ■ ■ WHAT NEXT?

On January 18, 1930, poet Rabindranath Tagore paid Gandhi a visit. He asked him what he had in mind for India. Gandhi did not know. "I am furiously thinking night and day," he replied, "and I do not see any light coming out of the surrounding darkness."

Congress had declared January 26 to be Purna Swaraj Day. In cities and towns, thousands of people recited a declaration of independence to show their support for swaraj. "We believe that it is the inalienable right of the Indian people, as of any other people, to have freedom and to enjoy the fruits of their toil and have the necessities of life so that they may have full opportunities of growth," the declaration read. The declaration

Gandhi *(left)* visits with Rabindranath Tagore in India in 1940. Tagore, a world-famous poet, and Gandhi had been friends for years.

went on to spell out how British rule had ruined India economically, spiritually, politically, and culturally. Celebrations in support of the swaraj movement were held that day in faraway cities such as Los Angeles and London, and wherever Indians had made their homes around the world.

The push for independence in India was making regular headlines in U.S. newspapers. Gandhi had become a well-known, though often misunderstood, figure. He was "a gnome of a man," reported Upton Close in the *New York Times* in January 1930. Though nearly naked in his dhoti, wrote Close, Gandhi "can be a menace to an empire." Close described how Gandhi, through the use of love, respect and self-sacrifice, had brought together millions of people despite their differences. He had broken with Hindu tradition by insisting that untouchables be treated as equals. He created a new name for them, saying it was wrong to call any humans untouchable: Harijan, or Children of God. Yet, "the masses worship him as a god," said Close. Gandhi's career, he wrote, "demonstrates what he teaches, that love can be the greatest practical force in the world."

Back in India, Gandhi had yet to decide on a plan for civil disobedience. His associates were worried. "I could tell them nothing," wrote Gandhi, "as I myself knew nothing about it. But like a flash it came, and as you know it was enough to shake the country from one end to the other." Salt would be the focus of this all-important campaign. "It is the formula of which I have been in search these long and weary months," said Gandhi. The campaign would target the hated British salt tax and salt monopoly.

Many people found Gandhi's decision baffling. They wondered why he didn't opt for something more dramatic. A fellow nationalist suggested instead a march on the viceroy's house. Someone else suggested establishing a parallel, all-Indian government.

But Gandhi was firm. "Next to air and water, salt is perhaps the greatest necessity of life," he said. "The salt tax oppresses all alike— Hindu, Mohammedan [Muslim], Parsee, Christian, Jew," he wrote in *Young India*. "It hits the poor man hardest, whatever be his religious persuasion." The British salt monopoly was so far-reaching that it even affected the country's cows. Indians could not so much as let their cattle lick salt from the beach without risking punishment. Gandhi deplored this British monopoly that forbade Indians from making their own salt. According to *Time* magazine, "Although India has four of the world's best rock salt areas . . . the British government dumps some 600,000 tons [544,000 metric tons] of British salt in the Indian market annually."

Gokhale, who had been such a strong influence on Gandhi, had been outspoken against the salt laws. British prime minister MacDonald himself had spoken against the salt laws. "The payers of the salt tax have no more to say on the Indian policy than the man on the moon," he remarked. All the same, after the Great War, the British government proposed an increase in the salt tax. Every Indian member of India's legislature voted against the increase. The government enacted it anyway. This decision proved "that Indian public opinion counted for practically nothing where British financial interests were concerned," wrote C. F. Andrews in the *New York Times*.

> "There is no article like salt outside water by taxing which the State can reach even the starving millions, the sick, the maimed and the utterly helpless. The tax constitutes the most inhuman poll tax that the ingenuity of man can devise."
>
> —Mohandas Gandhi, Young India, February 27, 1930

THE SALT MARCH TAKES SHAPE

Gandhi fondly remembered the Great March, which had been so effective in South Africa against the laws that denied Indians their rights. Marches and pilgrimages (religious journeys) were a cherished tradition in Gujarat. For this reason, Gandhi proposed to lead a group of followers on a march to the Arabian Sea to protest the salt laws. Upon reaching the sea, he would scoop up salt. By doing so, he would break the salt laws and signal the people of India to embark on acts of civil disobedience.

The idea of a salt march was brilliant in its simplicity. Yet even a brilliantly simple plan needs proper execution to succeed. Gandhi, his fellow nationalists, and the members of his ashram got busy.

There were many details to work out. Who would do the marching? What route would they take? When and how long would it be? Would the marchers bring their own food? Where would they sleep each night? To be successful, the planners also needed to launch a public education campaign about the salt laws and satyagraha. The press needed to be notified. So did the viceroy.

In early March 1930, Gandhi sent Lord Irwin a lengthy letter telling him of his plan to violate the salt laws. He wrote that he would willingly call off his plan if Irwin gave him sufficient reason to. Irwin sent back a simple reply: "His Excellency . . . regrets to learn that you contemplate a course of action which is clearly bound to involve violation of the law and danger to the public peace." The march was on.

When Gandhi announced his plan publicly, people from all over India wrote to him, eager to join the march. Gandhi, however, knew his marchers needed to be properly trained in nonviolent civil resistance. He needed to know that, come what may, they would conduct themselves honorably. For these reasons, he drew most of his marchers from the Sabarmati Ashram. These ashramites had had extensive training in the methods of satyagraha. They would know how to conduct themselves if officials resorted to violence and intimidation.

Gandhi proposed a march of a few days. His close associate, Sardar Vallabhbhai Patel, pushed for a longer march. A long march would help the campaign to build momentum and attract publicity. It would also give Gandhi more opportunities to educate the people about the salt laws and civil disobedience. Gandhi agreed. The proposed march would last nearly a month.

They began to plot out a route. The march would leave from the ashram, just north of Ahmadabad. The destination would be the small coastal village of Dandi. Dandi was home to ample salt deposits and villagers who knew how to gather salt. They could teach the practice to others. In the stops in between, Gandhi would speak to local peoples about the evils of the British salt laws and how to conduct oneself as a

Sardar Vallabhbhai Patel joined Gandhi's movement in 1917 and by 1930 was a close associate of Gandhi.

satyagrahi. He would encourage them to boycott British cloth and take up spinning. He would collect resignations from local Indian officials who held positions of authority in the British government. And while he was at it, he would stress the importance of good sanitation and the acceptance of untouchables—all the elements of the independent India he envisioned.

Sardar Patel planned the stops between Ahmadabad and Dandi. The route would cover approximately 240 miles (386 km). The marchers would stop in Hindu villages, where the people would be most receptive to Gandhi's message. Many Muslims felt left out of the nationalist movement, so they were less likely to rally round the marchers. By visiting villages where response would be the most enthusiastic, Gandhi could expect to draw bigger crowds and recruit more people for civil disobedience. Patel also knew the importance of involving the press in Gandhi's march, so he tried to choose villages with good channels of communication.

Timing was key. The marchers would leave the ashram on March 12. They would arrive in Dandi during National Week, when Indians commemorated the Amritsar massacre of April 13, 1919.

To help prepare the Indian people for the campaign, Gandhi published articles in *Young India*. In these pieces, he quoted the penal section of the Salt Acts (the parts that spelled out punishments for violating the act). He published a lengthy list of rules for satyagrahis.

SWALLEY HOLE AND DANDI

It could be argued that the British Empire's reign in India began and ended in very nearly the same place. Back in 1611, the British East India Company set up its first trading bazaar at Swalley Hole, on the coast of the Arabian Sea just northwest of Surat. The end of British rule began in 1930 at Dandi, just a few miles south of Swalley, when Gandhi picked up a muddy handful of salt to begin the massive civil disobedience that eventually led to Indian independence.

First and foremost, he stressed nonviolence as the key to the success of the campaign. He published an article titled "When I Am Arrested," telling the people how to proceed in the very likely event of his own arrest.

Students from the university in Ahmadabad formed an advance team, known as the Army of the Dawn. Their job was to travel ahead to all the places the marchers would stop. They arranged sleeping quarters for overnight stops, made arrangements for feeding the marchers, and found locations where Gandhi would speak.

Shortly before the march, Gandhi issued more instructions. Each village was to provide him specific information upon his arrival. What was the population of the village, broken down by sex and religion and number of untouchables? How many spinning wheels were there, and what was the monthly sale of khadi? Was there a school? How many children, boys and girls, attended? Gandhi also laid out rules about food. Villagers were to go to no expense to feed the marchers but stick to the simplest of foods. "For me goat's milk, if available, in the morning, at noon and at night, and raisins and dates and three lemons will do," he wrote.

▨ ▨ ▨ THE BRITISH RESPONSE

As the start of the march drew near, the British showed little concern. To many of them, Gandhi's plan simply seemed odd. Some found the idea of a salt march downright ridiculous. According to one British newspaper, "It is difficult not to laugh, and we imagine that will be the mood of most thinking Indians."

Nonetheless, in early March, officials arrested Sardar Vallabhbhai Patel in the village of Ras. Ras lay along the march route, and Patel had gone there to speak to the villagers about Gandhi's march and civil disobedience. Perhaps Gandhi would be arrested next.

CHAPTER 5

THE
SALT
MARCH

You must be the change you
wish to see in the world."

—Mohandas Gandhi, n.d.

On the evening of March 11, 1930, the city of Ahmadabad, India, was uncharacteristically quiet. The people who normally thronged the streets had gathered north of the city, near Gandhi's ashram. It was the eve of the Salt March. Approximately ten thousand people had gathered on the sandy bank of the Sabarmati River to hear Gandhi speak. They had come not only from Ahmadabad but from all over the country.

Gandhi appeared before the crowd. "In all probability this will be my last speech to you," he began. "Possibly these may be the last words of my life here." Should that happen, Gandhi continued, the march was to go on without him, as was civil disobedience. But he reminded his followers, "Let no one commit a wrong in anger."

He explained how to break the salt laws, once he gave the signal in Dandi. He reminded his audience to boycott foreign fabrics, take their children out of government schools, and resign their government positions. Picket shops that sold liquor, he said.

He asked everyone's involvement, not just the men's. "There are women who can stand shoulder to shoulder with men in this struggle," he added. And all satyagrahis needed to understand that they might end up in jail. But, Gandhi assured them, "Our ranks will swell and our hearts strengthen, as the number of our arrests by the Government increases."

Gandhi retired to the ashram for the night. He wrote a letter to Jawaharlal Nehru. If he were arrested that night, he wrote, the march would continue nonetheless. Then, without the slightest worry, Gandhi slept.

Outside, virtually nobody else slept. The mood of the crowd was excited but tense. The mere sound of a vehicle heading toward the ashram triggered anxious looks. Surely this was a police car coming to arrest Bapu and take him to prison. But the night passed, and Gandhi remained free.

THE MARCH BEGINS

Early on the morning of March 12, Kasturbai placed a garland of

Gandhi *(center, hatless)* and fellow protesters march toward Dandi on the first day of the Salt March, March 12, 1930.

khadi thread over Gandhi's head. She rubbed tilak, a dot of red paste, on his forehead as a blessing and mark of farewell. A supporter handed him a tall, lacquered bamboo staff. The seventy-eight marchers, including Gandhi's son Manilal and his grandson, Kantilal, had gathered outside the ashram's weaving factory. Every marcher was dressed in white khadi. They carried their belongings—bedding, spare clothes, and mugs—in packs on their backs.

An enormous crowd waited restlessly in the chilly air for the march to begin. They gathered around fires for warmth. Gandhi glanced at the large watch pinned to his dhoti. Ever punctual, at 6:30 A.M. on the dot, he began to walk, starting off at the same hour that he had begun the Great March in South Africa. He led the seventy-eight marchers through the gates of the ashram, faced his fellow Indians, and declared, "I would rather die a dog's death than return to the ashram a broken man."

As many as one hundred thousand people crowded the sides of the dusty road to Ahmadabad. They threw money. They filled the air with loud cracks as they split open coconuts for good luck. A band began to play "God Save the King," Great Britain's national anthem. Suddenly, the musicians caught themselves. This march was about independence from Great Britain. The sounds of the anthem ebbed away.

As Gandhi and the marchers disappeared toward Ahmadabad, many of the ashramites who were staying behind cried. They feared they would never see their beloved leader again. Gandhi's assistant, Mirabehn, remembered the sense of desolation. "Those of us who were

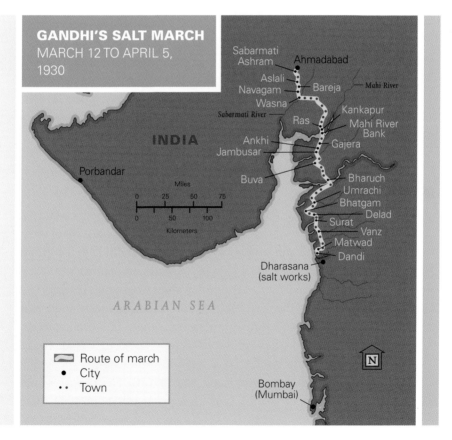

GANDHI'S SALT MARCH
MARCH 12 TO APRIL 5, 1930

Sabarmati Ashram
Ahmadabad
Aslali
Navagam
Bareja
Mahi River
Wasna
Sabarmati River
Kankapur
Ras
Mahi River Bank
INDIA
Ankhi
Gajera
Jambusar
Porbandar
Buva
Bharuch
Miles
Umrachi
0   25   50   75
Bhatgam
Delad
0   50   100
Surat
Kilometers
Vanz
Matwad
Dandi
Dharasana
(salt works)

ARABIAN SEA

Route of march
• City
•• Town

N

Bombay
(Mumbai)

left stood watching and watching," she said, "till there was nothing left to see but the cloud of dust hanging over the road."

Huge crowds along the route to the city were making it difficult for the marchers to pass. Onlookers, bicycles, cars, and trucks jammed the road. Gandhi intentionally walked faster to get through the throngs as quickly as possible. The large crowd did not fool him. "Many had come out just because others had done so," Gandhi wrote later. Their appearance at the march "was the beginning and end of their self-sacrifice."

Many people followed Gandhi and the marchers beyond Ahmadabad. He told the crowds to go home and do their part for independence. By then he was so dusty that some people failed to recognize him. Kasturbai had walked through the city with Gandhi, but now they parted. She headed back to the ashram.

Reporters were on hand to tell the story of the march to the world. According to the *Washington Post*, on March 13 Gandhi had "set forth on the crusade that Indian leaders have likened to Paul Revere's ride [to warn American colonists that the British were on the march in 1775]." How, the writer asked, would Great Britain respond to his campaign of civil disobedience? India, he noted, "is seething with unrest." If the British arrested Gandhi, it could spur a violent revolt.

THE FIRST WEEK

Once the march began, Gandhi and his followers provided a walking, talking example of how to behave as a satyagrahi. The marchers were to be self-disciplined and simple in their needs. Gandhi kept the group to a strict schedule. They were to spin a certain amount of yarn each day. In the face of violence or arrest, they were to offer no resistance.

Gandhi also used the march to illustrate the independent India that he envisioned: a united country, embracing people of all religions, in which every citizen, including untouchables, was treated as an equal. An independent India would be a self-sufficient country in which people plied the spinning wheel and wore khadi. The people would reject liquor and adopt healthy sanitation practices. He brought these lessons to every town he visited.

After the commotion at the outset of the march, the first day's march was typical of the days that followed. By late morning, the marchers reached the village of Aslali, home to more than fifteen hundred people. The villagers greeted the marchers with dancers and musicians playing flutes, cymbals, and drums. Gandhi's grandson had been carrying his bags, but as they neared the town, Gandhi saw a villager lugging them instead. A satyagrahi did not expect others to serve him. Gandhi retrieved his bags and, for the rest of the march, carried them himself.

Late that afternoon, approximately four thousand people gathered to hear Gandhi talk about satyagraha and the evils of the salt laws. "We shall prepare salt, eat it, sell it to the people, and while doing so, court imprisonment, if necessary," he said. After the meeting, the marchers collected donations, enrolled volunteers in satyagraha, and accepted resignations from villagers who held government jobs. The marchers ate a simple dinner: *khichri* (split peas and rice), *ghee* (clarified butter),

Gandhi speaks at an evening meeting during the Salt March. Large groups of people greeted the marchers at most every stop and listened to Gandhi speak.

milk, and buttermilk. They did their spinning and rested. Gandhi gave interviews. At 7:15 P.M. sharp, it was time for the evening prayer meeting. At 9:00 P.M., it was lights out.

Despite their exhausting first day, the group rose right on schedule, at 4:00 A.M. on March 13. Morning prayers took place at 4:20, and breakfast was at 5:00. By 6:00 A.M., all but two of the marchers were on their way. (These two could not find their sandals and left a half hour later.) The group reached the village of Bareja later that morning. Bareja's leader was sympathetic to the British, and Gandhi's speech drew only a small gathering. When a villager presented information about the village, Gandhi learned that nobody in Bareja wore khadi or spun.

Gandhi wrote letters in the afternoon. At 6:00 P.M., as the temperatures began to cool, the group marched to their evening destination, the village of Navagam.

The march followed this pattern in the days to come. The group walked in the early morning, rested during the hottest part of the day, and walked to that evening's destination in the late afternoon. At night they slept at *dharamsalas*, or village inns, instead of in private homes. That way, there would be no retaliation against homeowners who might welcome them. Each village visit provided Gandhi with an opportunity to lead by example.

On the third day of the march, the group was scheduled to spend the afternoon in the village of Wasna. Just outside of town, the residents had erected a cottage for Gandhi, a canopy for the marchers, and a temporary

WALKING AND WRITING

It wasn't enough for Gandhi to march an average of 12 miles (19 km) a day over dusty roads in the Indian heat. He also kept up a heavy writing schedule. He wrote regular letters and articles, and on March 24, 1930, he produced seven articles for *Young India*.

kitchen in a grove of mango trees. They seemed to have gone to great trouble to welcome the satyagrahis, but Gandhi was skeptical. His marchers included untouchables. He wondered if this elaborate preparation was intended to keep them out of town. In his speech that day, Gandhi was blunt. "If you have made the arrangement to avoid the untouchables entering the dharamsala, I would certainly be sorry," he said. "If you really want to assist me in the Swaraj propaganda, you cannot act in this way."

The reception from villagers the first week was largely positive. Thanks to the Army of the Dawn, every town knew when to expect the marchers. Often the townspeople sprinkled the road into their village with water to keep down the dust. Musicians greeted the marchers, and the townspeople threw flower petals in their path. The crowds that gathered to see Gandhi sometimes numbered in the ten thousands.

Many of the marchers struggled during those difficult first days. Said one marcher, the first week was marked by "unbearable heat . . . hot gusts of wind, . . . [and] flies." Some marchers fell sick and had to catch up with the group later. A number of them had trouble meeting their spinning quota. Gandhi essentially told them to try harder. Despite being the oldest marcher at sixty years old, he was faring as well as any of them. He had a long-standing tradition of making Monday a day of silence. He upheld the tradition during the march and made every Monday a day of rest.

Many people, including Gandhi, had expected his arrest at any time. Yet day after day passed, and he remained free.

■ ■ ■ CROSSING THE MAHI

At the end of the first week, the satyagrahis arrived in the village of Kankapura on the Mahi River. Kankapura was small, yet thousands of people gathered to hear Gandhi speak that night. He stood beneath a banyan tree as he addressed the crowd. After the speech, the marchers planned to cross the Mahi River. The best way to do this was by boat during high tide, which would come at about 11:00 that night.

At 10:30 P.M., Gandhi began his trip by boat from the north bank of the river. But as the boat left the shore, hundreds of people splashed into the river and tried to climb aboard. When the excited masses finally calmed down, the tide had ebbed. Gandhi and the marchers were forced to abandon the stranded boat. They waded the rest of the way across the shallow river through the thick, deep mud. There was no moon that night, so throngs of people along both shores carried torches to light the way. Gandhi and the others did not reach the south bank until 1:00 A.M.

Since Gandhi had started marching, the INC leaders had continued to make plans. Jawaharlal Nehru noted, "All our leading men and women at the center, as well as in the provinces and in local areas, were bound to be arrested. Who was then to carry on?" The All-India Congress Committee, the governing body of the INC, was scheduled to meet in Ahmadabad to appoint leaders and assign powers in the event of arrests.

Before the meeting, Nehru needed to consult with Gandhi. He traveled to Kankapura to meet him, but he arrived too late. Gandhi had already crossed the Mahi. The tide was still too low to cross the river by boat. "Never mind the mud and the ebb!" Nehru exclaimed. "I am young! I shall walk across!" He strode into the water and sloughed through the mud to the opposite side. The next day, he marched with Gandhi and consulted with him until a driver came to pick him up.

■ ■ ■ ■ WALKING THE WALK

Gandhi and the marchers were in the second week of their trek to Dandi. While they had received mostly enthusiastic receptions from villagers during week one, the reception varied in the days that followed. Some towns gave them a rousing welcome. In others, Gandhi drew only small crowds. Nonetheless, he was steadfast in his message: be ready to break the salt laws, wear khadi, boycott liquor, unite for independence, and treat one another as equals. All along the march route, he had opportunities to practice what he preached.

For many Indians, Gandhi's insistence that untouchables be treated as equals was asking nearly the impossible. All their lives, they had been taught to avoid untouchables. Gandhi put the beliefs of his Indian followers to the test. On March 21, the marchers arrived in the village of Gajera.

In the town of Buva, on March 23, a woman ran toward Gandhi to apply tilak to his forehead. Gandhi would not let her because she was wearing foreign-made cloth. If she really wanted to help him and the cause, he told her, she would wear khadi. Villagers recall that, after that day, she always wore homespun cloth.

More than four thousand people gathered to hear Gandhi speak. He sat on the platform they had provided and said nothing. He knew the people of Gajera had refused to allow untouchables to join the crowd. Finally, Gandhi spoke. "Either you invite the untouchables . . . to sit freely among you," he said, "or I'll have to address you from the hill where they are sitting." Finally the crowd agreed to integrate—though one report notes that more than one hundred people left rather than sit with untouchables.

At every village, Gandhi accepted resignations from Indians working as government officials. In some villages, however, the people had put immense pressure on these officials to force them to resign. In Ankhi, for example, Gandhi learned that the villagers there were retaliating against government officials by refusing them water. Satyagrahis did not act this way, Gandhi explained. "If [the officers] are really dying of hunger or thirst, it is not our dharma [moral duty] to let them perish in either manner."

Meanwhile, as Gandhi drew nearer to Dandi, the INC planned for the days ahead. A group of young INC members made a trip to Dandi before Gandhi's arrival. They found government workers trying to destroy the salt deposits in an attempt to thwart Gandhi's plan. But the coast stretched for miles, and salt was everywhere. The tide that washed in and out every day easily undid the workers' attempts.

The members of the All-India Congress Committee in Ahmadabad set up a chain of command in anticipation of arrests. They assigned new powers to local congressional leaders. Members of Congress, including Sarojini Naidu and Jawaharlal Nehru, then caught up with Gandhi in the village of Jambusar. Jambusar turned out to be a good stop for the marchers. The town's population of twelve thousand was about one-third Muslim. This might have meant a lower turnout for Gandhi's speech. Yet, approximately five thousand people showed up, including about one thousand Muslims.

Gandhi met with the congressional leaders. "We spent a few hours with him there," Nehru wrote, "and then saw him stride away with his party to the next stage in the journey to the salt sea." Nehru watched him go, "staff in hand, marching along at the head of his followers, with firm step and a peaceful but undaunted look."

■ SELF-PURIFICATION

After nearly two weeks on the march, Gandhi continued strong in his self-discipline. His marchers and his supporters, however, found self-discipline harder to maintain. They had agreed to live and eat simply, but they often accepted treats from the villagers. As for the villagers, Gandhi had asked them to offer only simple foods and amenities. Instead, they did what good hosts do and rolled out the welcome mat.

As the march went on, the failure of the marchers and villagers to stick to Gandhi's plan became a problem. On March 26, the

Sarojini Naidu *(right)* joins Gandhi briefly on the Salt March.

marchers arrived in the relatively large town of Bharuch. A doctor offered two of the marchers ice cream. They accepted. When Gandhi found out, he was not pleased. Ice cream was an extravagance. With the press paying close attention to the marchers, what message would it send if they were seen eating ice cream?

A similar problem arose two days later when the marchers reached the village of Umrachi. Umrachi was a poor village that was suffering a drought. It had only a few cows, so the villagers hired a car to bring in milk for Gandhi. Gandhi was appalled. He asked why they were going to such expense when their own people were hungry. He was equally displeased to learn that the villagers had shipped in mangoes, grapes, and other fresh fruits and vegetables for the marchers.

On the evening of March 29, the marchers reached Bhatgam. On the way to the village, Gandhi saw that a servant was carrying a heavy kerosene lantern on his head to light the path. When Gandhi walked faster, a local official prodded the servant to keep up. For Gandhi the plight of the servant was the last straw. That evening Gandhi directed his wrath not at the British but at his marchers, his supporters, and himself.

"You know, the common rule is to see our own big lapses as tiny nothings," he began, barely controlling his temper. "We profess to act on behalf of the hungry, and naked and the unemployed," he reminded them angrily. "I have no right to criticize the viceregal [British governor's] salary if we are costing the country . . . the average daily income of our people." He asked that he and his marchers repledge themselves to purity and simplicity.

Then he turned his attention to the villagers and their heavy lamps. "These lights are merely a sample of the extravagance I have in mind," he said. "In your hospitality towards servants like us, I would have you be miserly rather than lavish. . . . Extravagance has no room in this campaign." And certainly, Gandhi continued, no one was to be made a servant in the name of satyagraha. The servant with the lantern "was a humiliating sight," Gandhi said. "This man was being goaded to walk fast. I could not bear the sight." Better, Gandhi said, for one of the marchers to have carried the lamp.

THE LAST WEEK

Gandhi's harsh words worked their magic on the marchers. During the last week of the journey, they showed renewed purpose, self-discipline, and vigor. The next night, in Delad, the marchers carried the lamps. The group had been walking for well over two weeks, often under strenuous conditions, but they seemed more energetic than ever. Even Gandhi wrote that walking is "justly called the prince of exercises."

> "And today the pilgrim [Gandhi] marches onward on his long trek. Staff in hand he goes along the dusty roads of Gujarat. . . . And whither [where] go you, young men and women of India who shouted so loudly and so lately of Independence. . . . Whither go you?"
>
> *Jawaharlah Nehru, March 1930*

Gandhi would reach Dandi and begin civil disobedience in less than a week. Sardar Patel had urged Gandhi to plan for a long march to build up enthusiasm, momentum, and publicity. The wisdom of his advice was clear as the march reached Surat. Thousands of people joined the marchers as they approached the city. Another ten thousand more waited at the city's bridge. Trains arrived at the station, "crowded with white-clad enthusiasts," wrote Newton Phelps Stokes II, an American observer.

Approximately eighty thousand people poured into Victoria Gardens, where Gandhi was to speak. Clearly, his message about foreign cloth was catching on. The crowd was dressed almost entirely in khadi. That week the local khadi store had sold out its stock. As Gandhi waited on the platform for the crowd to settle, he "pulled out some corded cotton, a little hand spindle, and set to work, seemingly as oblivious of his surroundings as any craftsman in his shop," wrote Stokes.

Gandhi continued spinning as he spoke to the immense crowd. He urged them to boycott foreign cloth and live in harmony. The crowds remained after Gandhi had finished speaking. The next morning, when Gandhi and the marchers set out, the crowds were still there. They lined the streets and congregated on balconies to watch the marchers pass. They watered the dusty street so heavily that it was slippery in spots.

Enthusiastic throngs continued to turn out in the villages beyond Surat. The crowds included Muslims and women. A villager in Vanz asked Gandhi for a message. He replied, "Ply the spinning wheel, wear khadi, boycott liquor and cooperate in breaking the salt law." It was his recipe for Indian independence in one simple sentence.

DANDI

Early on the morning of April 5, the marchers set out on the last leg of their journey. They left the village of Matwad for Dandi, just 4 miles (6.5 km) away. Soon they could hear the sea. Then, all around them, they noticed salt left by the tide.

After an hour's walk, they reached the coastal village of Dandi. "Never was there a more forlorn setting for a drama than the tiny, straggling village of Dandi," wrote a reporter for the Associated Press (a U.S. news-gathering organization). "A distant ribbon of white moving across the dark mud flats was all that indicated the approach of Gandhi and his followers this morning."

Dandi was a small, very poor village located a difficult 10-mile (16 km) walk from the nearest train station. The town had very few resources. Gandhi worried that an influx of people would be too much for the villagers. "I would request you not to follow me there," he said in a speech prior to his arrival. "If you do, come as soldiers carrying your food on one shoulder and water on the other."

Sarojini Naidu arrived along with other congressional leaders. So did thousands of supporters. Some of them solved the water shortage by setting up water stations along the road into town. The international press was there as well. Gandhi granted interviews that afternoon.

Gandhi's Salt March offered important lessons for future civil disobedient movements around the world.

1. Set an example. Gandhi once said, "You must be the change you want to see in the world." By making an example of himself and the marchers, he offered a model of the India he envisioned.

2. Organize. The Salt March was successful, in large part, because of extensive advance planning.

3. Notify authorities. A satyagrahi operates fairly and out of love. According to this principle, Gandhi firmly believed that a satyagrahi had to notify authorities before staging civil disobedience.

4. Notify the press. Civil disobedience has minimal impact if the rest of the world is unaware of it. When the press can report on and explain acts of civil disobedience, their reports can create wider sympathy for the movement and, thus, bring greater pressure for change on the parties under challenge (in India's case, the British government).

5. Get women involved. This lesson seems obvious, but it hasn't always been so. Gandhi recognized that women were a powerful untapped resource in working for change.

When an Associated Press reporter noted that he had not yet been arrested, Gandhi admitted he was "wholly unprepared for this exemplary noninterference by the government." The British, he believed, had held off arresting him because they were "sensitive to world opinion."

That night in Dandi, Gandhi stood beneath a banyan tree and spoke to a large crowd. "Tomorrow we shall break the salt law," he told them. He very likely would be arrested. But he trusted civil disobedience to continue. "This movement is based on the faith that when a whole nation is roused and on the march, no leader is necessary." He urged his listeners to follow him in breaking the salt laws. After all, he reminded them, "You have a mine of salt right at your doorsteps." Independence, in other words, was theirs for the taking.

CHAPTER 6

GANDHI BREAKS THE SALT LAWS

" I want world sympathy in this battle of Right against Might."

—Mohandas Gandhi, April 5, 1930

On the morning of April 6, 1930, Gandhi emerged from a bungalow in Dandi. Four thousand people awaited him outside. First, Gandhi entered the sea to cleanse himself, as was customary following a pilgrimage. He waded far into the shallow water and then returned to the beach. Sarojini Naidu and others joined him. There, on the dark Dandi sand, the long-awaited moment had arrived. Gandhi reached down and scooped up a clump of mud and salt. "With this salt I am shaking the foundations of the empire," he said. Gandhi had broken the salt laws.

At this point, police easily could have swooped in and arrested Gandhi. He had broken the law. But he remained free and had given the signal. Civil disobedience could begin.

The volunteers on the beach were ready. In orderly groups of six, they began to draw water from the sea. Taking the water to a camp, they boiled it down to leave only the salt. The local people also got to work. A London Times reporter saw more than one hundred fifty people in a dry creek bed, "busily engaged in scraping salt from the deposits, piling it in mounds, and finally carrying it off in bags."

Gandhi *(see arrow)* and his followers walk to the seashore at Dandi on April 6, 1930.

Some claim that when Gandhi scooped up the salt, Sarojini Naidu exclaimed, "Hail, deliverer!" Actually, she greeted him as Law-Breaker. A famous photograph of Gandhi, Naidu, and others shows Gandhi stooping down to pick up salt (see page 5). The photograph is usually said to have been taken the moment that Gandhi broke the salt laws, but it is really a later reenactment.

Later that day, police seized the salt, which amounted to nearly 1,000 pounds (450 kilograms). After they left, the volunteers went right back to work.

Gandhi quickly issued a press statement. Since he had broken the salt laws, he wrote, anyone could do the same. They had to understand, however, that they could face arrest. If someone knew how to manufacture salt, he said, that person should instruct others, as long as they also explained the risk of prosecution.

In his statement, Gandhi urged Indians to boycott foreign cloth. He concluded with a special message concerning women. The women "can make a larger contribution than the men towards the attainment of independence," he said. "I feel they will be worthier interpreters of non-violence than men, not because they are weak, as men in their arrogance believe them to be, but because they have greater courage of the right type and immeasurably greater spirit of self-sacrifice."

He also sent a cable to the United States that appeared in national newspapers. He knew "countless friends in America" sympathized with India's independence movement. Sympathy was not enough, however. He asked for "expressions of public opinion" in favor not only of Indian independence, but of the movement's nonviolent approach. He concluded, "If we attain our end through nonviolent means, India will have delivered a message for the whole world."

■ ■ ■ CIVIL DISOBEDIENCE BEGINS

After Gandhi gave the signal, it "seemed as though a spring had been suddenly released," wrote Nehru. Civil disobedience had begun, and "salt-making was spreading like prairie fire." All along the coast, and in salt-rich areas such as Orissa, civil resisters were making salt. *Young India* published instructions on how to manufacture it. In cities and towns across India, people bought and sold salt illegally, often in packets boldly marked "Contraband [Illegal] Salt." In Ahmadabad, protesters opened an illegal salt store. Within two hours, they had made more than one thousand sales.

Nehru, like so many others, had been skeptical when Gandhi first proposed the salt campaign. With its success, he and his fellow doubters felt a bit silly for failing to see the campaign's potential, and they eagerly took part. Nehru, who had grown up in affluence, free of manual labor, happily dirtied his hands to make salt. He and his compatriots enthusiastically "collected pots and pans and ultimately succeeded in producing some unwholesome stuff, which we waved about in triumph and auctioned for fancy prices." On April 14, he was arrested for violating the salt laws and sent to prison for six months.

The police were nearly as busy as the salt makers. They were making arrests and seizing contraband salt. The jails began to fill up as the

INDIA IN 1930

In 1930 India's population was 340 million. This was one-fifth of the total world population and three times the population of the United States. The British ruled India with just 2,000 British officials and 60,000 British troops. In other words, there was one British soldier for each 5,500 Indian civilians. Added to this were 160,000 Indian troops and a police force made up mainly of Indians.

An Indian policeman disperses a mob of civil protesters in July 1930 using a lathi, or metal-tipped pole.

number of arrests increased. They arrested Gandhi's son Manilal and Mahadev Desai, Gandhi's personal secretary. In Bombay three hundred policemen raided the headquarters of the Indian National Congress. They found salt pans on the roof, full of evaporating salt water. They destroyed them.

"Salt in the hands of satyagrahis represents the honour of the nation," Gandhi wrote in *Young India*. "It cannot be yielded up except to force." In many instances, police did use force to seize salt. The Indian National Congress received troubling reports from all over the country. Police had used batons and lathis on salt makers. They had even poured boiling saline (salt water) on some of them.

But there were disturbing incidents of violence by resisters too. Riots broke out in Calcutta. In some places, resisters caused train derailments and detonated homemade bombs. According to one report, in Chittagong, a group of insurgents (rioters) raided the armory (a warehouse of military equipment) and made off with a cache of weapons. The Chittagong raid implied that some Indians had no plans to remain nonviolent.

In Peshawar, in the northwestern part of the country, police arrested several popular movement leaders. Riots broke out. The situation was so volatile that British women and children were evacuated. British officers shot into a crowd without warning, leaving hundreds dead and wounded. The government called in reinforcements. But two rifle platoons of Indian soldiers refused orders to fire on their unarmed compatriots. "The civil disobedience thereby became military mutiny," noted the New York Times.

Civil disobedience went beyond breaking the salt laws. Indians boycotted foreign cloth. They set fire to heaps of British-made textiles. In Delhi the city's tailors refused to sew foreign cloth.

Gandhi had asked women to participate in the movement, and they had responded with enthusiasm. "They came out in large numbers from the seclusion of their homes," wrote Nehru, "and, though unused to public activity, threw themselves into the heart of the struggle." Women arranged boycotts. They picketed liquor stores and joined marches. Even the British press noticed. Women, "thousands of them, many being of good family and high educational attainments," were joining the movement, noted a government report. They started going to jail, just like the men.

Through April, Gandhi remained free. The government, it seemed, was afraid to make a martyr of him by arresting him. Better to jail his key associates than to seize Gandhi himself.

■ ■ ■ THE PRESS AND THE SALT THIEF

All in all, the civil disobedience movement had become a massive force in India, and the international press was paying attention. But it was difficult to know which news stories to trust. The British controlled the cable wires over which all news came in and out of the country. If they felt a story was anti-British, they banned or censored it. Articles in the New York Times from this period make repeated references to riots and mob scenes. They refer to the satyagrahis as malcontents. Was that the view of the Times or the censors?

At the time of the Salt March, the majority of Indian women had never been involved in public or political life. They concerned themselves primarily with their homes and families. What's more, few women were educated, particularly compared to men. Gandhi was the first leader to reach out to the women of India and see their potential. Throughout the salt campaign, he appealed to women to organize among themselves for independence. In particular, he saw in them a potent force in boycotting foreign cloth and the anti-liquor campaign. His ashram conducted a training program for female satyagrahis that included instruction on how to run meetings, first aid, and spinning. Gandhi spoke about women's solidarity and emphasized the crucial role women could play in the independence movement. Women responded enthusiastically to Gandhi's call (*below, in Surat in April 1930*). They could be found throughout cities picketing shops that sold liquor or foreign cloth. A group of them wrote a letter to the viceroy explaining their motives for their involvement. Many went to jail. For most women, it was the first time they had ever participated in any political activity. Gandhi had opened the eyes of the women of India to their own power and potential.

The British government also tried to control the Indian press by imposing a press ordinance. Under the ordinance, all journals and newspapers were to pay a security deposit. Then, if a publication printed something that the government considered subversive, the publisher lost the security deposit and had to cease publication.

Gandhi refused to pay the deposit for the press that handled *Young India*. He urged other publishers to do likewise. There were ways around the government ordinance, he said. "For instance, I may dictate the contents of one issue to fifty men at a time and distribute the copies to fifty persons," he explained. Using the same method, those fifty people could dictate to another fifty people, and so on.

On April 26, Gandhi gave a speech at Charwada. Charwada lay within view of the Dharasana Salt Works. Huge salt mounds marked this large British-controlled salt operation. Gandhi said that people were calling him Salt Thief instead of Mahatma. "I like it," he said. How much of a thief was he, he asked, for taking salt from the sea and salt flats of his own country? "It will be real theft only when we raid those mounds of salt over there," he announced. The next step, he said, was to seize the saltworks. He himself would lead the raid. His announcement proved to be the tipping point for the British government.

GANDHI'S ARREST

On the evening of May 4, Gandhi began a letter. "Dear Friend," he wrote, addressing the viceroy, Lord Irwin. He wrote that he planned, with his supporters, to take over the large salt works at Dharasana. As with the Salt March, he was giving the viceroy a chance to respond in advance. He set the letter aside and went to sleep. He awoke soon after to find a flashlight shining in his face. A magistrate (judge) stood above him, surrounded by armed policemen.

"Are you Mohandas Karamchand Gandhi?" asked the magistrate. When Gandhi said yes, the officer explained he had come to arrest him. Gandhi asked for time to wash and clean his teeth. As he did so, he asked under what charges he had been arrested. The magistrate explained he was being charged under Regulation XXXV of 1827. The regulation dated back to the days of the East India Company, a time of far more arbitrary laws. Under this regulation, no trial would be necessary for Gandhi, not even a sentence. He simply would be held at "the pleasure of the Government" for as long as they saw fit.

By this time, Gandhi's supporters had joined him. Gandhi gave his assistant, Mirabehn, his letter for the viceroy. The group sang a hymn and prayed. Then the officials shouldered their arms and whisked Gandhi away by truck. They put him aboard the Frontier Mail, a red and yellow train bound for Bombay.

Just outside of Bombay, the train screeched to a halt at a small station. The police had arranged to have Gandhi taken off the train here. Two intrepid journalists, including Negley Farson of the *Chicago Daily News*, had learned that Gandhi would be stopping there and hurried to report on the transfer. When the train abruptly halted, explained Farson, "hundreds of turbaned heads popped out of the windows to see what was up."

Under guard, Gandhi stepped off the train. Farson was able to speak to "this wizened . . . holy man." He asked, "Have you any farewell messages, Mr. Gandhi?"

"Tell the people of America to study the issues clearly and to judge them on their merits," Gandhi said. Within minutes a British officer led Gandhi to a waiting Buick. Wrote Farson, "Forty horsepower created in Detroit [Michigan] whisked the Mahatma from our sight on what will be the last ride in liberty that he will know for some time."

The news of Gandhi's arrest swept through India. The people responded with hartals, demonstrations, and meetings. Webb Miller, a U.S. journalist, witnessed thousands of people in khadi marching through the streets of Bombay. "The procession flowed slowly along for miles like a white river," he wrote. Most of the participants in the demonstrations were Hindu. Jinnah had discouraged Muslim participation. Still, some Muslims joined the demonstrations.

Around the world, people responded to Gandhi's arrest. In places as far apart as Panama in Central America and Kenya in Africa, Indians closed their businesses. In the United States, more than one hundred

A procession of people through the streets of Bombay protests the arrest of Gandhi in 1930.

clergy members sent Prime Minister Ramsay MacDonald a cable. They begged him "to seek the way to an amicable [friendly] settlement with Gandhi and his people." Like many others around the world, they wondered how MacDonald, with his background of pacifism and reform, could arrest Gandhi.

The arrest of Gandhi under Prime Minister MacDonald's watch "is one of the major tragedies of our era," wrote A. J. Muste, a U.S. social activist. "For Ramsay MacDonald, who a dozen years ago was hunted by mobs through British cities for his opposition to war, now to throw a great fellow-pacifist in jail and to countenance [support] violent measures for breaking up a campaign of non-violence, marks the breakdown of an outstanding personality which leaves his friends powerless to say a word in his defense."

THE DHARASANA SALT RAID

Ideally, a satyagrahi sought to change an opponent's mind by appealing to that person's morality. Sometimes this approach worked. For example, Chicago reporter Farson saw an official savagely beating a resister with a lathi. The resister, a Sikh, was a big man, said Farson, and made no effort to fight back. "He was hit until his turban came undone and his topknot was exposed," wrote Farson, referring to the traditional Sikh headwear and hairstyle. Soon he was bleeding, but he stood there, hands at his side, through the beating. The policeman drew his arm back, ready to take one more swing, then suddenly stopped. "'It's no use,' he said, turning to [Farson] with an apologetic half grin. 'You can't hit a [fellow] when he stands up to you like that.' He gave the Sikh a mock salute and walked off."

Gandhi was in prison, but the raid he had planned on the Dharasana Salt Works went forward. Taking Gandhi's place as leader of the raid was Sarojini Naidu. On May 21, she gathered with her fellow satyagrahis near the Dharasana works. U.S. journalist Webb Miller arrived as they assembled. He found more than two thousand satyagrahis in their white homespun, awaiting orders.

Naidu began with a prayer. She said, "Gandhi's body is in jail but his soul is with you." She reminded them of their duties as satyagrahis: "You must not use violence under any circumstances. You will be beaten but you must not resist."

The raid began with a line of men stepping forth from the throng of satyagrahis. Among the leaders was Manilal, Gandhi's second son. They began to advance on the salt mounds, which were guarded by four hundred riflemen and policemen carrying steel-tipped lathis. As the marchers drew near, police ordered them to leave. They cited a new regulation that prohibited gatherings of more than five people. The column of men continued, undaunted, toward the salt.

Satyagrahis prepare to raid the Dharasana Salt Works on May 21, 1930. The raid was led by Sarojini Naidu because Gandhi was in prison.

"Suddenly, at a word of command," recounted Miller, "scores of native police rushed upon the advancing marchers and rained blows on their heads with their steel-shod lathis. Not one of the marchers even raised an arm to fend off the blows. They went down like tenpins. From where I stood I heard the sickening whacks of the clubs on unprotected skulls . . . . In two or three minutes the ground was quilted with bodies.

"We did not conquer India for the benefit of the Indians. We conquered India as the outlet for the goods of Great Britain. We conquered India by the sword, and by the sword we should hold it."

—William Joynson-Hicks, Conservative Party leader in Great Britain, October 1930

Great patches of blood widened on their white clothes." When the police had beaten down every marcher in the column, another column of marchers assembled. They began to advance on the saltworks, knowing full well what was in store for them. They, too, were beaten savagely, and so it continued. As one line of marchers was beaten, another line stepped forward to take its place. The beatings went on and on.

"Finally the police became enraged by the nonresistance," wrote Miller. They began kicking the men and dragging them into ditches. "Hour after hour stretcher-bearers carried back a stream of inert, bleeding bodies."

Miller was speaking with Naidu when a British officer appeared. The officer touched Naidu on the arm and said, "Sarojini Naidu, you are under arrest." Naidu "haughtily shook off his hand and said: 'I'll

"For many generations the British treated India as a kind of enormous country house (after the old English fashion) that they owned. They were the gentry owning the house and occupying the desirable parts of it, while the Indians were consigned to the servants' hall, the pantry, and the kitchen.... We [Indians] developed the mentality of a good country-house servant. Sometimes we were treated to a rare honor—we were given a cup of tea in the drawing room. The height of our ambition was to become respectable and to be promoted individually to the upper regions. Greater than any victory of arms or diplomacy was this psychological triumph of the British in India."

—*Jawaharlal Nehru, 1941*

come, but don't touch me.'" She was soon sentenced to nine months in prison. Manilal Gandhi was sentenced to a year's imprisonment.

After the raid, a statement by the British government reported only a few serious injuries. Miller managed to bypass the British censors, and his story of the Dharasana raid appeared in 1,350 newspapers worldwide. It was read aloud in the U.S. Senate. People around the globe, including many British, were horrified.

In India the account made Indians angry yet proud. Nonviolence "was slowly undermining British rule," wrote journalist William Shirer. "It was filling them [Indians] with hope that some day, and soon, they would again be masters in their own country."

CHAPTER 7

THE
END
OF THE
RAJ

"In forty years of struggle I have frequently been told I was attempting the impossible, but invariably I have proved the contrary."

—Mohandas Gandhi, interview with George Slocombe, *New York Times*, May 1930

By May 1930, virtually all the leaders of the civil disobedience movement were in prison, along with thousands of other satyagrahis. Estimates of the number in prison range from sixty thousand to one hundred thousand. Gandhi, for one, found prison restful after the clamor and struggles of the prior months. He spent his time reading, writing, spinning, and sewing. Nehru, on the other hand, found it frustrating to be behind bars. He longed to be on the outside, working for the cause.

The effects of civil disobedience rippled through India and elsewhere. The boycott of foreign cloth was so widespread that in Britain, "mill after mill has closed its doors indefinitely," according to the press. Indian women continued to be active participants in civil disobedience. Overall, the movement had given Indians a sense of empowerment.

In June the Simon Commission released its report. It had been more than two years since the all-British commission had visited India and stirred protests among Indians furious at being denied any place on the commission. Finally, the commission was releasing its findings and recommendations for government reforms.

The commission released the report in two parts. The two-part release was a signal that the commission knew its findings would be unpopular. Part 1 of the report outlined what the commission members saw as India's homegrown ills. In particular, they detailed the problems of the caste system, tensions among India's various religious sects, and the reluctance of the princely states to be part of a united India. With so much division and enmity, the report argued, India required a strong central government such as the British were providing.

Part 2 of the report, released soon after, recommended that the British continue in their role as that strong central governing body. The commission suggested that under the British, India move gradually toward self-government as a federation of self-ruling provinces. Each province would have its own government, just as in the United States each state has its own state government.

The report "makes it plain on almost every page, that Britain does not intend to relax her control," noted the *New York Times*. "Despite all its emphasis on self-rule for the provinces, the scheme is to give Britain a stronger hold on India than ever." The people of India rejected the report as insulting. One Indian newspaper described it as "an atrocious document," another as "Simon's sorry folly." Both Hindus and Muslims condemned the report. Mohammed Ali Jinnah called the recommendations "reactionary [ultraconservative], short-sighted and petty-minded."

The Simon Report recommended that the British retain tight control over India. Nationalists, such as Gandhi and Nehru, wanted complete independence. Lord Irwin still held out the possibility of dominion status. Back in December, he had proposed a round table conference to discuss this option. In July, on the heels of the Simon Report, he confirmed that the British remained ready to discuss dominion status at the conference.

THE FIRST ROUND TABLE CONFERENCE

In November 1930, more than eighty Indian and British delegates convened in London, England, for the Round Table Conference. They gathered in the posh Royal Gallery of the House of Lords (the upper house of the British Parliament). Representing India were princes and maharajas (rulers) from the princely states, Muslim leaders such as Mohammed Ali Jinnah, Hindu leaders, and untouchables. But not a single member of the Indian National Congress attended. Congressional members boycotted the conference. It was not dominion status they sought but complete independence. They wanted no part in discussing a lesser option.

King George V opened the proceedings with a brief speech. The king welcomed the delegates to "the capital of my Empire." He then left the hall, and Prime Minister Ramsay MacDonald spoke.

"We are now at the very birth of a new history!" MacDonald announced. He pointed out that they had gathered on this momentous occasion to discuss "India's advancement within the companionship of the Commonwealth." Also in attendance were the prime ministers of the dominion countries of Australia, Canada, and South Africa.

Delegates meet in the Royal Gallery of the House of Lords (British Parliament) in London, England, for the first Indian Round Table Conference in 1930.

For all the pomp and flourish at the opening of the conference, the delegates could accomplish little. Without any representatives from the Indian National Congress, the conference was like "a wedding without the bride," said one reporter. Nonetheless, several interesting developments came out of the gathering.

First, contrary to the Simon Report, the Indian princes announced that they were willing to join a federation of princely states and British India. As a result, the British government said that if India were to form a federation, Great Britain would be willing to grant reserved dominion status. Under reserved dominion status, Britain would control the country's military, foreign affairs, and finances. Indians would control everything else.

Australia, Canada, and South Africa all enjoyed full dominion status. They were in charge of their own military, financial, and foreign affairs. The British were offering India a lesser status. Still, the delegates discussed how such a federation would work. The greatest sticking point was how to protect the interest of minorities, particularly Muslims and untouchables.

The Round Table Conference concluded its discussions in January 1931. On January 19, Prime Minister MacDonald announced that there would be a Second Round Table Conference in the fall to conduct further negotiations. He invited congressional members to participate. He announced that if the civil disobedience movement were called off, the government would release India's fifty thousand political prisoners.

■ ■ ■ ■ THE GANDHI-IRWIN PACT

Civil disobedience in India had continued nonstop from the moment Gandhi broke the salt laws on April 6, 1930. Most of the movement's leaders had spent the rest of the year in prison. Nehru had been out of jail for all of eight days in October 1930, when police arrested him for another act of sedition. All over India, protesters staged no-tax campaigns, hartals, and boycotts. Indians saluted their national flag rather than Britain's Union Jack. The government fought back with beatings, censorship, and arrests. Reports poured into *Young India* of police violence and mistreatment of prisoners, some mere children. The year 1930 had been brutal and turbulent.

Prime Minister MacDonald finally thought it might be possible to negotiate an end to the strife. On January 25, 1931, the government released Gandhi from prison. Soon after, at Gandhi's request, Gandhi and Lord Irwin began a series of meetings. They held long, intense talks at the viceroy's palace in New Delhi, India's capital city.

Journalist William Shirer wrote, "It was a sight . . . to see the Mahatma clad in his loincloth and an old blanket wrapped around his shoulders, trudging in his clumsy wooden sandals up the marble steps of the great palace past the scarlet-coated guards standing stiffly at attention." While Shirer was awed, old-guard British officials were not. Winston Churchill (who would later become the British prime minister) said it was "nauseating" to see this "seditious [treasonous] fakir [Muslim holy beggar] striding half-naked up the steps of the Viceroy's palace," to negotiate on equal terms with the viceroy.

As the talks progressed, Gandhi consulted regularly with members of the Congress Working Committee. Well-to-do Indian merchants also weighed in, requesting an end to civil disobedience. The merchants had been funding the movement all these months, and they were broke, their businesses in shambles. Lord Irwin, meanwhile, kept up a steady exchange of communication with officials in London.

There were many details to work out. In exchange for an end to civil disobedience, the British agreed to release all nonviolent political prisoners. Boycotts of British goods would end. The British would return confiscated property to resisters. Indians who had refused to pay taxes would once again pay them. Gandhi and Irwin discussed finer points of negotiation too. They discussed exactly what word to use to end civil disobedience. "Suspended," Irwin felt, was not the right word. It sounded as if civil disobedience would start up again at the slightest provocation. They settled on "discontinued."

Although both sides made trade-offs, the Indians made far more than the British. For example, the British refused to abolish the contentious salt tax. But they did agree that individual Indians would be allowed to collect or make salt for their own use, including for their livestock. They could also sell it within their villages. Finally, it was decided that Gandhi alone would represent the Indian National Congress in the Second Round Table Conference.

The end result of the negotiating was an agreement called the Gandhi-Irwin Pact. Gandhi and Lord Irwin signed the pact on March 5, 1931. After the signing, Lord Irwin had tea brought in. Gandhi had a small bag of salt tucked away in his shawl. He sprinkled a bit of it into his cup. "I will put some of this salt into my tea to remind us of the famous Boston Tea Party," he quipped.

> **"You have not got so many clothes on, you know, that you can afford to leave any behind."**
>
> —Lord Irwin, after Gandhi left the Gandhi-Irwin Pact signing without his shawl, March 5, 1931

Many Congress members felt horribly let down by the pact. They had embarked on civil disobedience expecting the triumphant end to be complete independence. When Nehru saw the agreement, he found it a "tremendous shock. . . . Was it for this that our people had behaved so gallantly for a year? Were all our brave words and deeds to end in this?"

Gandhi, very likely, had hoped to accomplish more. He had at least expected the British to suspend the salt laws. Nonetheless, with the Gandhi-Irwin Pact, Gandhi had achieved a milestone in Indian history. The pact marked the first time a British official had negotiated with an Indian, face-to-face. Up until then, the British government had simply dictated to Indians.

Gandhi is greeted by fellow passengers aboard the S.S. *Rajputana* on his way to England, on August 29, 1931, for the Second Round Table Conference.

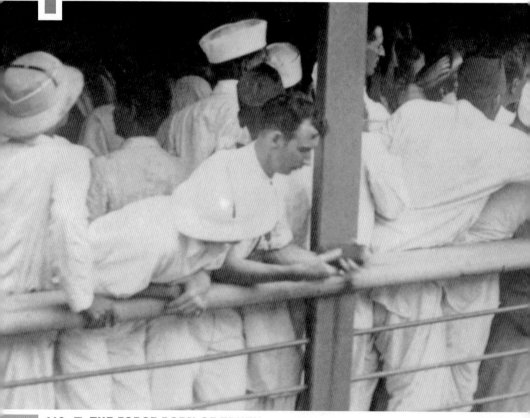

■ GANDHI GOES TO GREAT BRITAIN

On August 29, 1931, Gandhi sailed from Bombay for Great Britain, bound for the Second Round Table Conference. He was representing the Indian National Congress, and he had but one agenda: complete independence for India. In his bit of luggage, he carried a copy of Thoreau's *Civil Disobedience*. His youngest son, Devdas, traveled with him.

Gandhi's arrival in September generated great excitement. Crowds of people came to see him disembark his ship. Newsreels show him arriving in London on a chilly, wet day, clad in his usual dhoti, shawl, and sandals, and cheered by throngs of well-wishers. Throughout his stay, which lasted into December, people clamored to see him. On his walks through the city, he chatted with passersby. British children called him Uncle Gandhi, a sign of affection.

While in London Gandhi made a radio broadcast to the people of the United States. It was the first time his voice had been broadcast in this nation. His first words to Americans were: "Do I have to speak into this thing?" The rest of his twenty-minute speech was more inspiring. "I have no hesitation whatsoever in inviting all the great nations of the earth to give their hearty cooperation to India in her mighty struggle," he said.

While his reception among the British was warm and welcoming, he found tougher going at the Second Round Table Conference. He was the sole representative of the Indian National Congress, which wanted independence for India. The British were determined to maintain their hold. They allowed no discussion of granting India dominion status.

Gandhi *(wrapped in shawl)* attends the Second Round Table Conference in London in 1931.

In November 1931, a London schoolboy was late returning to class after lunch. When his teacher asked for an explanation, he said that he had stopped to watch a meeting between Gandhi and Charlie Chaplin, a famous actor. The teacher was aghast. How dare he make up such a tale! She proceeded to give him a thorough caning as punishment. The boy probably did see Gandhi with Chaplin. They met at Chaplin's request.

Instead, the delegates spent their time drafting a new constitution for the country. Many delegates argued for giving minorities, including Muslims and untouchables, special electoral privileges (proportional representation). Gandhi argued that in an independent India everyone was to be equal in every way. He was firmly against such privileges.

Ultimately, the Second Round Table Conference ended with no agreement. Gandhi left Britain on December 5. He arrived in Bombay at the end of the month. By this time, the British had declared the INC to be illegal, and Gandhi and Nehru were sent back to prison. Indians wondered if the Salt March and the civil disobedience campaign had made any difference at all.

Yet Jawaharlal Nehru later wrote, "Nineteen-thirty had, indeed, been a wonder year for us, and [Gandhi] seemed to have changed the face of our country with his magic touch. No one was foolish enough to think that we had triumphed finally over the British Government. Our feeling of elation had little to do with the Government. We were proud of our people, of our womenfolk, of our youth, of our children for the part they had played in the movement. It was a spiritual gain, valuable at any time and to any people, but doubly so to us, a subject and downtrodden people. And we were anxious that nothing should happen to take this away from us."

With the Salt March, Gandhi had empowered the people of India. He had made them understand that they need never again think of themselves as inferior. They were a force greater than they had ever suspected.

THE RAJ CRUMBLES

After the failure of the Second Round Table Conference, Gandhi took a step back from wrangling with the British. He focused instead on improving India from within by developing village industries such as spinning and weaving. He worked to improve sanitation and sought equality for untouchables.

At the same time, the rift between Hindus and Muslims in India widened. Under a new law, the 1935 India Act, Indians could for the first time vote for their provincial leaders. In the first provincial elections in 1937, Hindus representing the Indian National Congress dominated the results. (One notable exception was the heavily Muslim province of Bengal, which elected a Muslim government.) Muslims felt shut out as the elected leaders from the INC appointed other Congress members to government posts. Mohammed Ali Jinnah warned that if the British were to leave, Muslims would fall under the control of a Hindu Raj. Membership in the Muslim League soared.

WORLD WAR II

Beyond India, global troubles were leading to the outbreak of World War II (1939–1945). On September 3, 1939, Britain declared war on Germany. As part of the British Empire, India also declared war on Germany. Without having any say in the matter, Indians were called upon to fight, just as they had in World War I.

To the east of India, the Imperial Japanese Army was advancing across Asia, where Great Britain had other colonies. In early 1942 the Japanese held approximately one hundred thousand British troops, most of them Indian, as prisoners of war. More than half of these troops were captured when Singapore, a British military stronghold, fell to the Japanese in February 1942. Having seized Singapore, Japanese soldiers were making their way across Burma (present-day Myanmar) to the east of India. India would surely be their next target. The British army was already spread thin fighting in both Europe and in the South Pacific. How could they possibly defend India as well?

Gandhi believed the only way for India to save herself from Japanese attack was for the British to declare India independent. In 1942 nationalists under Gandhi's leadership launched the Quit India movement—a campaign calling for the British to quit (leave) India. Protesters staged nonviolent demonstrations and strikes. Large numbers

Indians demonstrate during the Quit India movement in 1942.

Members of the Quit India movement try to avoid government tear gas in Bombay in 1942.

of Indians broke with Gandhi's call for nonviolence, however. They destroyed railroad stations, telegraph lines, and government buildings. British response was swift and harsh. Gandhi and other movement leaders, including Nehru and Sarojini Naidu, were jailed almost immediately. So was Gandhi's wife, Kasturbai.

BEAT IT?

Nationalists debated what slogan to use for the civil disobedience movement of 1942, the goal of which was Indian independence. One suggestion was for the British to "Get Out." Gandhi felt those words were impolite, and they ultimately settled on "Quit India."

Gandhi and his fellow nationalists spent most of the rest of the war in jail. Gandhi was imprisoned in a palace along with Kasturbai. They were in their seventies and had been married since they were thirteen. Their marriage had developed into a devoted partnership. Kasturbai was so cherished by the Indian people that they called her Ba, the Hindi word for "grandmother."

In prison Kasturbai suffered a series of heart attacks. On February 27, 1944, she died, with Gandhi at her side. Gandhi was heartbroken. "I cannot even imagine life without Ba," he said. Gandhi was released from jail on May 6, 1944. Over the course of his life, he had served more than six years in prison.

Gandhi mourns at the deathbed of his wife, Kasturbai, in 1944.

Subhas Chandra Bose, born in 1897 in Orissa, worked for Indian independence alongside Jawaharlal Nehru and Gandhi. He was jailed many times. In 1938 he was elected president of the Indian National Congress. By this time, however, he had become impatient with Gandhi's nonviolent tactics. India, he said, must become fully independent immediately, by armed force if necessary. He resigned from a second term as the Congress president to form Forward Bloc, a party that sought independence by any means necessary.

In World War II, Bose saw an opportunity to expand his revolutionary independence efforts. He met with leaders of the Axis powers (Germany and other enemies of Great Britain and its allies), including Japanese officials. With their support, Bose recruited soldiers from India's civilian (nonmilitary) population as well as from the thousands of Indian prisoners of war held by the Japanese. Under Bose's command, the Indian National Army (INA), which numbered more than forty thousand soldiers, fought against the British in Southeast Asia.

In October 1943, in Singapore, Bose created the provisional government of Azad Hind, which means "Free India." He named himself both prime minister and minister of war and declared war on the Allies. In August 1945, when the Japanese surrendered to the Allies, the INA surrendered as well. Bose, who was known as Netaji (Leader), is believed to have died in a plane crash on August 18, 1945, in Taiwan. The circumstances of his death remain a matter of much dispute.

During this time, Jinnah was negotiating with the British. He saw that the British had to eventually leave India, and he wanted to safeguard Muslim interests in postwar India. Jinnah proposed the partition of India into separate Hindu and Muslim countries. He had a name for the new Muslim country: Pakistan. The name means "land of the Paks," the spiritually pure.

World War II ended in 1945. Great Britain and her allies had won, after a long, hard conflict. But as a result of the demands of the war, the British no longer had the resources or the will to stay in India. During the war, some of the Indian armed forces had mutinied (risen up against their leaders), and the British knew they would be unable to control India without the support of Indian troops. So, at long last, Great Britain agreed to grant India independence.

For years Gandhi had worked for this outcome. He had fasted and marched and given speeches from one end of the country to the other. Independence was on its way, but it was nothing like the independent India he had envisioned.

■ ■ ■ PARTITION

The British agreed to Mohammed Ali Jinnah's idea of a divided India. India would be partitioned—divided into two countries. India would be predominantly Hindu, and Pakistan (present-day Pakistan and Bangladesh) would be primarily Muslim, just as Jinnah had proposed. In August 1947, India became an independent country. Jawaharlal Nehru became the country's first prime minister. That same month, Pakistan also became an independent country. Mohammed Ali Jinnah became its first governor-general.

The partitioning of India broke Gandhi's heart. His dream of one India, embracing Hindus, Muslims, Christians, untouchables— Indians of all castes and religions—had not come to pass. Gandhi felt that he had failed. All his struggles, he said, "have come to an inglorious end."

The partition created incredible turmoil and violence, including fighting, looting, kidnapping, and murder. Hundreds of thousands

Muslim refugees cram into trains bound for Pakistan to escape the violence between Hindus and Muslims in New Delhi and other areas of India in 1947.

of people were killed in the months after the partitioning. Hindus committed atrocities against Muslims. Muslims committed atrocities against Hindus. Gandhi did all he could to bring calm. He traveled the country, praying, talking, and visiting the people. Finally, he announced a fast, willing to die if it would end the violence.

When he began his fast on January 13, 1948, he was nearly eighty. He soon became too weak to get up. Religious leaders hurried to his side with assurances of peace. On January 16, he ended his fast by sipping orange juice. He spoke from his cot. His voice was old and quiet. "I have no wish to live if I cannot see peace established all around me," he said.

FAREWELL

On January 30, 1948, Gandhi was ten minutes late arriving at a prayer meeting in New Delhi. He was still somewhat weak from his fast, but to Gandhi, that was no excuse. "I hate being late," he said. He hurried

Gandhi, weak from his fast, is helped as he leaves a Muslim shrine, in January 1948. He was murdered three days later.

to the prayer meeting. Five hundred Indians had gathered to hear him speak. Among them was a radical Hindu man who was enraged by Gandhi's calls for unity with Muslims, whom he considered the enemy. The man stepped out and shot Gandhi three times. "Oh, God," Gandhi murmured as he fell. He died soon after.

Jawaharlal Nehru announced the news on the radio. "Friends and comrades," he said, "the light has gone out of our lives, and there is darkness everywhere. . . . Our beloved leader, Bapu as we called him, the father of the nation, is no more."

BAPU, THE FATHER OF THE NATION IS NO MORE

The *Indian Express* announces the death of Gandhi in its February 1, 1948, edition.

All over the world, people mourned Gandhi's assassination. In South Africa, Prime Minister Jan Christiaan Smuts called Gandhi, "one of the great men of my time." U.S. president Harry S. Truman called the assassination an "international tragedy." Ed Snow, a U.S. journalist who had met Gandhi, wrote in the *Saturday Evening Post*, "This small man, so full of a large love of men, extended beyond India and beyond time."

His words were prophetic. As the years have passed, Gandhi has continued to inspire people around the world to work nonviolently for change, peace, and justice.

CHAPTER 8

"A MESSAGE FOR THE **WHOLE WORLD**"

If my faith burns bright, as I hope it will even if I stand alone, I shall be alive in the grave, and what is more, speaking from it."

—Mohandas Gandhi, n.d.

In October 1947, just months before Gandhi's assassination, the Reverend John Haynes Holmes of New York City visited Gandhi in India. Holmes had been one of Gandhi's earliest champions in the United States. In 1921, when Gandhi was virtually unknown to Americans, Holmes had given a sermon, "Who Is the Greatest Man in the World?" His answer was Mohandas Gandhi. Since that time, he and Gandhi had corresponded and become friends.

"Holmes, I have failed, totally failed," Gandhi told the minister that day in 1947. India was independent, yes, but it was not the India Gandhi had envisioned. His beloved country had been divided. Religious animosity had resulted in a tide of violence. Still, Holmes could not be convinced that Gandhi had failed. He tried to reassure him of all the good he had done.

Gandhi, after all, had given the world a great gift: a nonviolent method of effecting change. By that day in October, his legacy had already begun to unfold in the United States.

Indians in London read about the death of Gandhi on January 30, 1948. Men and women around the world mourned the leader's death.

JOURNEY OF RECONCILIATION

On April 9, 1947, eighteen young men—nine white, nine black—boarded interstate buses in Washington, D.C., bound for Virginia, North Carolina, Kentucky, and Tennessee. They planned to test a recent U.S. Supreme Court decision (*Irene Morgan v. Commonwealth of Virginia*) that banned racial discrimination in interstate travel. The young men wanted to see if Southern states, where segregation (separation of the races) was a way of life, would enforce the federal law as required.

The young men belonged to a new organization called the Congress of Racial Equality (CORE). CORE took its inspiration from the philosophy of Mohandas K. Gandhi. CORE organizers believed that Gandhi's nonviolent methods for overthrowing the British could be used to end segregation in the United States. They called their bus campaign the Journey of Reconciliation.

Southern officials were in no mood to reconcile with these young activists. In North Carolina, they arrested a number of the riders for violating local laws, which called for segregated bus seating. Bayard Rustin was among the men arrested. The authorities sentenced him to three months on a chain gang. Rustin, a committed Gandhiist, accepted his sentence as Gandhi would, with a smile. "If we got to go, we got to go," he said.

As Rustin went off to serve on the chain gang, Gandhi was still alive on the other side of the world. It is likely that Holmes told Gandhi about the Journey of Reconciliation when they met in October. Holmes had played a role in the founding of CORE. CORE's Journey of Reconciliation was just the first step in bringing satyagraha to the United States.

MONTGOMERY BUS BOYCOTT

The members of CORE did not limit their work to interstate buses and the South. They targeted segregated public facilities such as restaurants and swimming pools throughout the country, including in Los Angeles, California, and Denver, Colorado. Most of these campaigns were successful in integrating individual facilities. Still, the people at CORE knew that nonviolent action had the potential to end segregation on a massive scale. But their movement lacked a powerful spokesperson.

Rosa Parks (shown here shortly after her arrest) sparked the spread of the American civil rights movement by refusing to give up her bus seat in 1955.

Then, on December 1, 1955, in Montgomery, Alabama, a black woman named Rosa Parks refused to give up her seat on a city bus to a white person. When she was arrested for violating segregation laws, Montgomery's African American community launched a massive boycott of city buses in protest. For more than a year, black people refused to ride buses and walked or carpooled instead. A young minister, the Reverend Martin Luther King Jr., became the movement's leader. The Montgomery Bus Boycott was the first major campaign of the U.S. civil rights movement to use Gandhian methods. And in Dr. King, nonviolent action gained a powerful spokesperson.

King had learned about Gandhi from Mordecai Johnson, the president of Howard University, a historically black institution in Washington, D.C. King was drawn to Gandhi and his methods, and he wanted to learn how to employ nonviolent action. Bayard Rustin was among those who went to Montgomery to help train King and the other activists in Gandhi's methods.

King quickly embraced Gandhi's beliefs. "If we are arrested every day, if we are exploited every day, if we are trampled over every day, don't ever let anyone pull you so low as to hate them," he said during the boycott. "We must use the weapon of love."

After more than a year, during which blacks refused to ride Montgomery's city buses, the city agreed to desegregate public transportation. Civil rights activists had won their first major victory in the United States using Gandhian tactics.

John Haynes Holmes (1879–1964)

Holmes, a pacifist, was distressed by the "violence and hate" he saw in the outbreak of World War I. When Holmes read about Gandhi's work in South Africa, "Something clicked with me, like the turning of a lock," he said. By 1921 Holmes was publicly referring to Gandhi as the greatest man in the world.

Holmes helped found the Fellowship of Reconciliation (FOR), an interfaith peace organization. FOR leaders, including James Farmer, FOR's secretary for race relations, wondered if Gandhi's methods could be applied to racial problems in the United States. The answer, they suspected, was yes.

As a result, in 1942 they helped to form the Congress of Racial Equality, or CORE, to put Gandhi's nonviolent practices to work to end racial segregation. James Farmer became CORE's first national director.

Bayard Rustin (1912–1987)

One of CORE's earliest members was Bayard Rustin. Rustin, a pacifist, had served time in a penitentiary for refusing to serve in the military during World War II. Rustin and the other members of CORE began to use Gandhian techniques to challenge segregation. In 1947 Rustin was imprisoned in North Carolina for violating local segregation laws during the Journey of Reconciliation. After his release, he spent six months in India studying nonviolent strategy.

In 1951, in New York City, Rustin led a march to protest the Korean War (1950–1953). An outraged onlooker grabbed Rustin's placard and attacked him with it. Rustin gave the man a second stick to double his attack. It was Satyagraha 101: the man, disgusted, left the scene.

Rustin went on to be one of the key leaders in the civil rights movement. He provided early guidance on Gandhian techniques during the Montgomery Bus Boycott and organized the 1963 March on Washington.

James Lawson (1928–)

Lawson embraced nonviolence as a boy and became familiar with Gandhi as a teenager. He spent much of the Korean War in prison for refusing to serve in the military. Upon his release, he traveled to India to work as a Christian missionary.

In December 1955, Lawson read a front-page story in a local Indian newspaper. Blacks in Montgomery, Alabama, had launched a bus boycott to protest segregation. An inspiring young minister was leading the boycott. His name was the Reverend Dr. Martin Luther King Jr.

Later, back in the United States, Lawson met King. They found they shared a commitment to using nonviolent action. At King's request, Lawson went to the South to conduct workshops on nonviolent action, inspiring scores of young people to follow in Gandhi's footsteps.

THE CIVIL RIGHTS MOVEMENT TAKES OFF

After the Montgomery Bus Boycott, the U.S. civil rights movement swiftly gained momentum. Young people, particularly students, black and white, flocked to workshops on nonviolent methods. In Nashville, Tennessee, a young black minister, James Lawson, taught young activists the principles of nonviolent action. Students such as Diane Nash and John Lewis attended these classes faithfully.

In 1960, Lawson's students, including Nash and Lewis, put their lessons to work. At this time, lunch counters throughout the South refused service to African Americans. Black people were not allowed to take seats at the counters. Students challenged discrimination by holding peaceful sit-ins at lunch counters in Nashville, Tennessee, and in Greensboro, North Carolina. They sat at the counters and asked to be served. The students were challenging, in a nonviolent way, a law they knew was wrong.

As the students kept up the sit-ins, week after week, they drew the ire of white racists. Whites taunted them. They poured ketchup and mustard on the students. They beat up a white civil rights activist until he was bloody, a scene that was aired on national news. Not once did the students retaliate. By summer the lunch counters of Nashville and Greensboro were serving black customers.

An African American man—taunted by the white man on the right—practices nonviolent protest during the lunch counter sit-in in Greensboro, North Carolina, in 1960.

Gandhi's influence was again evident in the Freedom Rides of 1961. The Freedom Rides picked up where the 1947 Journey of Reconciliation left off. Black and white civil rights activists rode interstate buses through the South, challenging segregation in interstate travel. Just as Gandhi had notified Lord Irwin of his plans prior to the Salt March, the Freedom Riders notified authorities, including President John F. Kennedy, before they set out.

Two of the Freedom Riders were John Lewis and Diane Nash, veterans of the lunch counter sit-ins and students in James Lawson's nonviolence action workshops. In Jackson, Mississippi, authorities arrested Lewis and other Freedom Riders for violating segregation laws and sent them to the state penitentiary (prison) in Parchman. The prison issued them only olive green T-shirts and shorts. Some of the Freedom Riders complained. They wanted socks and long pants. Then

As part of a nonviolent protest, black Freedom Riders wait in a room reserved for white passengers in Montgomery, Alabama, in 1961.

one of their group exploded. "What's this hang-up about clothes?" he boomed. "Gandhi wrapped a rag around his [private parts] and brought down the whole British Empire!"

■ ■ ■ THE MARCH ON WASHINGTON

Through the early 1960s, the civil rights movement gained power and momentum. Activists staged marches, sit-ins, and swim-ins. They began campaigns to end segregation in hotels, restaurants, and swimming pools. Northerners went to the South, intent on helping to end segregation. Most of these efforts relied on nonviolent action to effect change.

The Salt March had been a turning point in the Indian independence campaign. In 1963 the U.S. civil rights movement staged a major march of its own, the March on Washington. This march aimed to promote improved job opportunities for African Americans and pushed for a national civil rights bill. At the rally in Washington, D.C., Martin Luther King Jr. delivered his "I have a dream" speech. Bayard Rustin, the longtime champion of Gandhian methods, was the chief organizer of the march. The march, and King's stirring speech, drew more Americans to the cause of civil rights.

DR. KING AND THE SALT MARCH

"If humanity is to progress, Gandhi is inescapable," Martin Luther King Jr. once said. The Salt March was his favorite Gandhi story, according to historian Taylor Branch. King would tell the story with gusto. When he described Gandhi picking up the salt in Dandi, King would exclaim, "It seemed I could hear the boys at Number Ten Downing Street [the British prime minister's residence and office] in London, England, say, 'It's all over now'!"

American civil rights leader Martin Luther King Jr. waves to the crowd during the historic March on Washington protest in August 1963.

In 1964 the U.S. Congress passed the Civil Rights Act making segregation in public facilities illegal. The term *satyagraha* had not caught on, but Gandhi's practices were making inroads into the entrenched racism of the United States.

SELMA

Civil rights activists turned to obtaining equal voting rights for African Americans. On March 7, 1965, John Lewis was among five hundred marchers who gathered in Selma, Alabama. They planned to march 54 miles (87 km) to Montgomery, the state capital, to advocate for African American voting rights.

As the march began, said Lewis, "there was no singing, no shouting— just the sound of scuffling feet. There was something holy about it, as if we were walking down a sacred path. It reminded me of Gandhi's march to the sea." The group reached the Edmund Pettus Bridge over the Alabama River. As they crossed the bridge, they saw, on the other side, "a sea of blue-helmeted, blue-uniformed Alabama state troopers, line after line of them," wrote Lewis. Behind the troopers waited the local sheriff's men, his posse, and mounted police. Suddenly, the troopers bore down on the marchers with clubs, whips, rubber hoses, and tear gas. They cracked Lewis's skull. They rode their horses over marchers. They brutalized them any way they could as white onlookers cheered.

The press was there too. That night the ABC television network interrupted its Sunday night movie to report what had happened in Selma. For fifteen minutes, viewers watched footage of the brutality. It was not the first time Americans had seen footage of racist violence against civil rights activists. "But something about that day in Selma touched a nerve deeper than anything that had come before," wrote Lewis. Bloody Sunday, as the day became known, echoed the raid at Dharasana.

Two weeks later, civil rights activists held another, much larger march. This time, the marchers, including John Lewis, went all the way to Montgomery. This march resembled the Salt March not only in the huge crowds it drew and the distance it covered, but also in its careful planning. Planners bought seven hundred air mattresses and seven hundred rain ponchos for the marchers. They made arrangements for food, lodging, physicians, and countless other details. Later that summer, on August 6, 1965, President Lyndon Johnson signed the Voting Rights Act.

Years later, John Lewis, by then a U.S. congressman, said, "The Selma-Montgomery March had a profound impact on the psyche of all Americans. It was like Gandhi's march to the sea. It transformed American politics."

SATYAGRAHA ALL OVER AGAIN

The similarities between Gandhi's salt campaign and the U.S. civil rights movement are striking. Both challenged a deeply entrenched opponent.

In the Salt March, Gandhi and his followers were taking on the most powerful empire in the world. Civil rights workers in the United States were facing down deep-rooted racism in the United States, particularly in the South.

Both campaigns attracted similar groups of volunteers. They both drew scores of educated young people who were not willing to tolerate the repression of the past. Women came out in force for both campaigns. In India, women flocked to Gandhi's cause. In the South, black women marched and organized and endured beatings. Many had never before been involved in any kind of political movement. Fanny Lou Hamer, for instance, was a sharecropper (poor farmer) in rural Mississippi. In her mid-forties, she became active in the voting rights movement. Ultimately, she became one of the movement's most inspiring leaders.

> "Nonviolent direct action seeks to create such a crisis and foster such tension that a community which has constantly refused to negotiate is forced to confront the issue."
> —Martin Luther King Jr., April 16, 1963

In India and in the South, activists became well acquainted with the rough side of nonviolence. Jail became a fact of life. U.S. civil rights activists endured beatings, just as the satyagrahis had. Most endured them just as Gandhi would have instructed, without resistance. The press was able to photograph many of these incidents. Their stories, pictures, and film footage appeared in newspapers and on the nightly television news. They influenced people's view of the movement. Public opinion turned against racism, just as it had against British rule.

In India some nationalists found satyagraha frustrating. They longed for a more radical approach. So it was in the U.S. civil rights movement.

Many young activists found Dr. King and his insistence on nonviolence, goodness, and love maddening. Malcolm X, a militant black activist, was one example. "The goal of Dr. Martin Luther King is to get Negroes to forgive the people who have brutalized them for 400 years," he said in 1963, something he found himself unable to do. He rejected the notion of nonviolence, particularly in the name of self-defense. Rather than passively endure brutality, he advocated fighting back.

GANDHI'S LEGACY FOR THE WORLD

When Gandhi died, a Briton named Philip Noel-Baker said, "Gandhi's greatest achievements are still to come." Gandhi's legacy has reached beyond the U.S. civil rights movement. It can be found in movements and struggles throughout the world. Here are just a handful:

- In South Africa, Desmond Tutu and Nelson Mandela took inspiration from Gandhi in their struggles to end apartheid, the legal separation of the races, and to introduce multiracial democracy in their country. Mandela became South Africa's first black president in 1994. Tutu won the Nobel Peace Prize in 1984. Mandela won in 1993.

- Gandhi is a key influence on Aung San Suu Kyi of Myanmar (Burma). Since the 1980s, Aung San Suu Kyi has challenged the country's repressive military regime and worked to reintroduce

Nelson Mandela and Desmond Tutu

Aung San Suu Kyi

democracy. Called the Burma Gandhi, she has been under house arrest almost constantly since the 1990s. She won the Nobel Peace Prize in 1991.

• Benigno Aquino Jr., who helped to end the dictatorship of Ferdinand Marcos in the Philippines in the 1970s, found inspiration in Gandhi. Aquino was assassinated in 1983 before he could carry out his plans, but he inspired Filipinos to use nonviolence to bring down the corrupt Marcos government.

• In Poland, Lech Walesa, the leader of Poland's Solidarity labor movement, relied on nonviolence to overthrow the country's Communist rule in the late 1980s. Walsea won the Nobel Peace Prize in 1983 and became the first non-Communist President of Poland since World War II.

• In the tiny republic of Lithuania, citizens used nonviolence. On March 11, 1990, they declared their independence from the Soviet Union, the first Soviet republic to take this bold step. In the days leading up to the declaration, Lithuanian television aired the movie *Gandhi* night after night to inspire its citizens.

Lech Walesa

Cesar Chavez used Gandhi's nonviolent methods to protest against unfair treatment of farmworkers in California in the 1960s and 1970s.

In the United States, Gandhi was also an inspiration to Cesar Chavez, founder of the United Farm Workers of America. Chavez used marches, boycotts, fasts, and picketing to advocate for farmworkers and their right to form unions. One of his earliest targets was California grape growers who refused to let workers unionize. In 1966 Chavez led a 340-mile (547 km) march from Delano, California, to the state capital in Sacramento to draw support from state legislators. He successfully called on millions of Americans to stop buying grapes. In 1968 Chavez went on a twenty-five-day hunger strike to emphasize the movement's commitment to nonviolence. Finally, in 1975, the grape growers agreed to allow workers to join the farmworkers union.

More recently, Gandhi's influence can be found in organizations such as Soulforce. Soulforce, which takes its name from the English translation of satyagraha, uses nonviolence to advocate for rights and acceptance for lesbian, gay, bisexual, and transgender people. Each year, Soulforce holds an Equality Ride. Groups of students bus to conservative

Christian colleges that disapprove of homosexuality. Their goal is to talk openly and bring greater awareness and acceptance of gay people.

■ CONCLUSION

Gandhi once said, "Nonviolence is the greatest force at the disposal of mankind." The Salt March illustrated the power of nonviolence so eloquently and effectively that it continues to inspire people years later. When the Selma-Montgomery marchers reached Montgomery, the Reverend Martin Luther King Jr. spoke to an enormous crowd. He quoted the "Battle Hymn of the Republic." "Mine eyes have seen the glory of the coming of the Lord," he said, his voice filled with emotion. "His truth is marching on!"

Dr. King was not referring to Gandhi. Still, the image of truth trudging faithfully forward conjures up Gandhi as Nehru described him in 1930: "The pilgrim marches onward on his long trek," he wrote. "Staff in hand he goes along the dusty roads of Gujarat." Gandhi's legacy has been so far reaching, and so long lasting, that it seems as if he is still marching those dusty roads. The world will long remember how, against enormous odds, one man, armed with nothing but the truth, picked up some salt and brought down an empire.

1600: Queen Elizabeth grants a charter on December 31 to the East India Company to claim territory for England in the East Indies.

1858: The British government takes control of India from the British East India Company. India becomes part of the British Empire.

1869: Mohandas K. Gandhi is born in Porbandar, in the province of Gujarat, India, on October 2.

1883: Mohandas Gandhi marries Kasturbai. Both are thirteen years old.

1888: Gandhi sails for England to study law.

1891: Gandhi, having been admitted to the bar in London, returns to India.

1893: Gandhi leaves India for South Africa in April to handle a legal case. In June, while riding in a first-class train compartment in South Africa, Gandhi experiences racial discrimination. He is ordered to move to third class and then taken off the train.

1894: Gandhi founds the Natal Indian Congress in South Africa.

1907: Gandhi conducts a satyagraha campaign in South Africa to protest the Transvaal Asiatic Ordinance, which requires Indians to register with the government and always carry a permit. Gandhi is sent to jail.

1913: Gandhi leads a satyagraha campaign in South Africa to protest laws that discriminate against Indians. More than two thousand men, women, and children participate in the Great March.

1914: South African general Jan Christiaan Smuts and Gandhi reach agreement on the Smuts-Gandhi Pact to protect the rights of Indians in South Africa.

1915: Gandhi and his family return to India.

1916: Gandhi attends the National Indian Congress at Lucknow. He meets Jawaharlal Nehru. Muslims and Hindus unite to sign the Lucknow Pact, pledging to set aside religious differences in the fight for independence from Britain.

1918: On November 18, World War I ends. More than one million Indians served with the British military during this war.

1919: On April 6, Gandhi calls for a nationwide strike to protest the Rowlatt Acts, which deny basic legal rights to political prisoners. On April 13, British general Reginald Dyer orders troops to fire on Indians meeting peacefully in Jallianwalla Bagh in the city of Amritsar. In ten minutes, Dyer's men kill nearly four hundred men, women, and children and wound more than one thousand in the Amritsar massacre.

1920–1922: Gandhi initiates a national noncooperation movement, maintaining it will result in self-rule for India. He calls off noncooperation when violence breaks out in Chauri Chaura.

1922: Gandhi is arrested, tried for sedition (treason), and sentenced to six years in prison.

1927: The British government appoints the Simon Commission to study the Indian government and recommend changes. Indian nationalists protest the exclusion of Indians from the commission.

1928: A committee of various Indian political parties releases the Nehru Report. The Nehru Report is intended to serve as the constitution for a self-governing India. Muslims condemn the report for failing to adequately protect Muslim interests. The Indian National Congress meeting in Calcutta in December gives Britain one year to grant India dominion status. Otherwise, the Congress will declare India independent and launch a massive civil disobedience campaign.

1929: The British fail to meet the December 31 deadline set by the INC. The Congress embarks on swaraj, a movement for complete independence from Britain.

1930: On March 12, Gandhi, along with seventy-eight followers, leaves his ashram near Ahmadabad to embark on a 240-mile (386 km) march to Dandi. On April 6, Gandhi breaks the British salt laws by scooping salt from the beach at Dandi. This action serves as the signal for the country to launch a massive civil disobedience movement. On May 4, Gandhi is arrested and imprisoned. On May 21, under the leadership of Sarojini Naidu, Gandhi's followers march on the Dharasana Salt Works. They suffer high casualties at the hands of the police. The story of the beatings appears in the press worldwide and creates sympathy for India's independence struggle. In November the First Round Table Conference is held in London, England. Members of the INC boycott the conference.

1931: Gandhi and Lord Irwin sign the Gandhi-Irwin Pact. The pact calls for an end to civil disobedience in exchange for concessions by the British government. Gandhi serves as sole representative for the INC at the Second Round Table Conference in London.

1935: The British Parliament passes the India Act of 1935, which grants Indians self-government at the provincial level but retains British control over the country's finances, military, and foreign affairs.

1942: Gandhi launches the Quit India movement. The movement results in widespread violence. Gandhi and other Congress leaders are imprisoned.

1944: Kasturbai dies in jail on February 22, with Gandhi at her side.

1947: The British partition India into independent India, which will be mostly Hindu, and Pakistan, which will be mostly Muslim. Jawaharlal Nehru becomes India's prime minister. Mohammed Ali Jinnah is Pakistan's governor-general.

1948: Gandhi is assassinated by a radical Hindu youth at a prayer meeting in New Delhi on January 30.

2007: The United Nations (an international organization devoted to world peace) declares October 2, Gandhi's birthday, an International Day of Nonviolence.

2010: Gandhi's granddaughter spreads some of Gandhi's ashes in the Indian Ocean off the coast of South Africa to mark the sixty-second anniversary of his death.

Kasturbai Gandhi

(1869–1944) Kasturbai Gandhi, born in Porbandar, India, married Mohandas Gandhi when they were both thirteen years old. After some early hesitation, she eventually embraced Gandhi's causes. She participated in satyagraha in South Africa, helped to promote spinning and better sanitation practices among Indians, and was an active satyagrahi in India. Affectionately called Ba, Hindi for "grandmother," she was imprisoned in 1942 and died in prison in 1944, with Gandhi at her side.

Mohandas Gandhi

(1869–1948) Mohandas K. Gandhi was born in Porbandar, India, on October 2. He was married at thirteen to Kasturbai and educated as a lawyer in Great Britain. In 1893 he traveled to South Africa to handle a legal case. Appalled by how Europeans treated Indians there, he fought for justice through the use of nonviolent civil disobedience. He called his method satyagraha, or Soul Force. He lived in South Africa for twenty-three years, ultimately using satyagraha to improve the rights of South Africa's Indians.

In 1915 Gandhi returned to India, where he used satyagraha to challenge British rule in India. In 1930 he led seventy-eight followers on a 241-mile (386 km) march to the coastal village of Dandi, where he initiated massive civil disobedience by scooping up salt and breaking the British salt laws. Soon Indians across the country were making and selling contraband (illegal) salt. While the salt campaign did not bring immediate independence from the British, it gave Indians a new sense of empowerment. In 1947 the British granted India independence as part of partitioning the country into Hindu India and Muslim Pakistan. The partitioning devastated Gandhi, who had always worked for Hindu-Muslim unity. Gandhi was assassinated by a radical Hindu on January 30, 1948.

Gopal Krishna Gokhale

(1866–1915) Born in Kotaluk, on the west coast of India, Gokhale was one of India's most influential early advocates for Indian self-rule and social reform. From the late 1800s until his death in 1915, he worked to improve Indian education, to unify Hindus and Muslims, and to bring greater political power to his fellow citizens. Considered a moderate, he mentored both Mohandas Gandhi and Mohammed Ali Jinnah.

Lord Irwin

(1881–1959) Lord Irwin, the viceroy of India during the time of the Salt March, was born Edward F. L. Wood in Devon, England. Lord Irwin was a deeply religious man, which the British government saw as an advantage when selecting him to be viceroy of India. The government felt he would be well suited to deal with Gandhi, for whom Indians felt spiritual reverence. It was under Lord Irwin's watch that the British arrested Gandhi in 1930 and also brutalized the Indians who participated in the raid on the Dharasana Salt Works. Yet it was also Lord Irwin who met face to face with Gandhi in 1931 to hammer out the Gandhi-Irwin Pact, which ended civil disobedience. Until then, no viceroy had ever met with an Indian on equal terms. Lord Irwin returned to Great Britain soon after the signing of the pact.

Mohammed Ali Jinnah

(1876–1948) Jinnah was born in Karachi, India (present-day Pakistan), and studied law in Great Britain. He was the leading advocate for protecting the rights of Muslims in India. He successfully campaigned for the British to partition India into two independent countries: India, primarily Hindu, and Pakistan, predominantly Muslim. Jinnah became Pakistan's first governor-general in 1947. Jinnah is known as the Father of Pakistan.

Sarojini Naidu

(1879–1949) Sarojini Naidu, born in Hyderabad, in the eastern Indian province of Andhra Pradesh, was one of India's leading poets before becoming active in the Indian independence movement. She met Gandhi through their mutual friend, Gopal Krishna Gokhale, and became one of Gandhi's most loyal supporters. In 1925 she became the first woman to serve as president of the Indian National Congress. She is often referred to as the Nightingale of India. While most people treated Gandhi with reverence, Naidu enjoyed bantering with Gandhi, whom she called the Mystic Spinner, and to whom she was devoted.

Jawaharlal Nehru

(1889–1964) Jawaharlal Nehru, born in Allahabad, India, was the son of a prominent Indian lawyer and nationalist politician, Motilal Nehru. He enjoyed a wealthy upbringing and attended prestigious schools in Britain, including Cambridge University. Upon his return to India, the Indian independence movement awoke his passion. Inspired by Gandhi and the noncooperation movement, Nehru became a leader of the Indian National Congress. While Gandhi insisted on the steady pace of nonviolent civil resistance, Nehru often longed for more radical approaches. Whereas Gandhi rejected industrialization, Nehru embraced it. Nonetheless, Nehru remained fiercely loyal to Gandhi. In 1947, when India was declared an independent country, Nehru became its first prime minister, serving until his death in 1964. Beginning in 1966, Nehru's daughter, Indira Gandhi, served four terms as India's prime minister before her assassination in 1984.

Motilal Nehru

(1861–1931) Born in Garden Grove, India, Motilal Nehru was a prominent, wealthy Indian lawyer and politician. He had spent his political career as a moderate in the INC until his son, Jawaharlal, became interested in Gandhi's noncooperation movement in 1920. Motilal was skeptical of Gandhi at first and concerned about his son's involvement in the civil disobedience movement. After the 1919 Amritsar massacre, though, Motilal Nehru embraced Gandhi and his movement and served time in prison for civil disobedience.

Bal Gangadhar Tilak

(1856–1920) Bal Tilak is known as the Father of Indian Unrest. He was born in Ratnigiri, in Maharashtra in western India. A scholar and journalist, he joined the Indian National Congress in 1890. He advocated a radical approach to Indian independence as opposed to the moderate approach embraced by INC leaders such as Gokhale. "Swaraj [self-rule] is mine, and I shall have it!" he said. To attain independence, he led boycotts against British goods. He pushed for better education as a path to independence and promoted Hindu-Muslim unity. The British imprisoned him twice, including a six-year sentence in Burma.

ashram: a religious community

bapu: the Hindi word for "father" and an affectionate nickname for Gandhi

caste: a person's place in society or social level. In the Hindu caste system, members of the Brahman caste hold the highest social position. Traditionally, the caste system determines a person's occupation and social circle. Untouchables, who prefer the term "Dalit," traditionally have been so low among Hindus that they fall below the caste system. The caste system was legally abolished in India in 1950, although it is still often unofficially observed.

dharamsala: a village inn, generally for travelers on a pilgrimage

dhoti: a loincloth for men

hartal: a strike

khadi: homespun cloth

lathi: a long, metal-tipped bamboo pole used as a weapon

Mahatma: "Great Soul," the name given to Gandhi by Indian poet Rabindranath Tagore

purna swaraj: complete self-rule

Raj: in Indian history, Raj is short for the British Raj, when India was under the rule of the British government. "Raj" is the Hindi word for "king" or "rule."

satyagraha: Mohandas Gandhi's philosophy of nonviolent action. In Satyagraha or "soul force," a person seeking change uses the forces of truth, nonviolent resistance, and love to appeal to an opponent's sense of morality.

satyagrahi: a person who participates in satyagraha

sepoy: an Indian who served in a European-controlled army. In India, sepoys served as soldiers for the East India Company and later for the British Indian Army.

swaraj: independence; literally "self-rule"

tilak: among Hindus, a mark (usually red) most often applied to the forehead. The mark can be applied as a blessing. Tilak on a woman can indicate that she is married.

5   Thomas Weber, *On the Salt March: The Historiography of Gandhi's March to Dandi* (New Delhi: HarperCollins India, 1997), 346.

6   Gandhi International Institute for Peace, "Essential Quotes of Mahatma Gandhi," 2008, http://www.gandhianpeace .com/quotes.html (January 5, 2010).

7   Mohandas K. Gandhi, *An Autobiography: The Story of My Experiments with Truth* (Boston: Beacon Press, 1957), 6.

7   Ibid., 4.

8   Ibid., 6.

8   Ibid., 13.

8–9 Ibid., 12.

9   Ramachandra Guha,"Gandhi and Cricket," *Hindu*, September 30, 2001, http://www .hinduonnet.com/2001/09/30/ stories/0730028p.htm (March 11, 2008).

15 Queen Victoria of the United Kingdom, "Proclamation by the Queen in Council, to the princes, chiefs, and people of India," November 1, 1858, Wikisource, August 22, 2008, http://en.wikisource.org/wiki/ Queen_Victoria%27s _Proclamation (January 6, 2010).

17 Gandhi, *Autobiography*, 20.

17 Ibid., 21.

17 Ibid., 22.

17 Ibid., 23

18 Lawrence James, *Raj: The Making and Unmaking of British India* (New York: St. Martin's Press, 1998), 349.

18 Ibid., 352.

20 Ibid., 53.

20 Ibid., 47.

20–21 Ibid., 68.

21 Ibid., 61.

21 Ibid., 81.

21 Ibid., 82.

22 Mohandas Gandhi, "Statement in the Great Trial," Wikisource, September 5, 2008, http://en.wikisource .org/wiki/Statement_in_The _Great_Trial (January 5, 2010).

23 Gandhi, *Autobiography*, 94.

23 Ibid., 94.

24 Ibid.

25 Ibid., 112.

25 Ibid., 115-16.

25 Ibid., 131.

26 Henry David Thoreau, *On the Duty of Civil Disobedience*, n.d., http://thoreau.thefreelibrary .com/Civil-Disobedience (March 11, 2008).

26 Gandhi, *Autobiography*, 299.

27 Ibid., 134.

27 Ibid., 137.

27 Ibid., 139.

27 Ibid., 140.

28 Ibid., 143.

29–30 IndiaLife History, "Lokmanya Bal Gangadhar Tilak," IndiaLife, 2007, http:// www.indialife.com/History/ freedomf_tilak.htm (January 6, 2010).

32 Gandhi, *Autobiography*, 298.

34 Mohandas Gandhi, "The Last Satyagraha Campaign: My Experience," *Indian Opinion*, Golden Number, December 1944, n.d., http://www .anc.org.za/ancdocs/history/ people/gandhi/1-4.htm#2 (December 29, 2009).

35 Mohandas Gandhi, *Collected Works*, vol. 20, 15.

36 Mohandas Gandhi, "What is Swaraj?" *Hind Swaraj*, n.d.,

http://www.mkgandhi.org/
swarajya/coverpage.htm
(March 11, 2008).

37 Leo Tolstoy to Mohandas
Gandhi, May 8, 1910, January
1, 2009, http://en.wikisource
.org/wiki/Correspondence
_between_Tolstoy_and
_Gandhi (March 11, 2008).

38 New York Times, "General Labor
War in South Africa," January
14, 1914, 4.

40 Jawaharlal Nehru, Toward
Freedom: The Autobiography of
Jawaharlal Nehru (New York:
John Day Company, 1941), 69.

41–42 Padmini Sengupta, Sarojini
Naidu: A Biography (New York:
Asia Publishing House, 1966),
88–89.

42 Ibid.

42 Ibid., 90.

42 Ibid.

45 Gandhi, Autobiography, 387.

45 Ibid., 395.

46 Ibid., 489.

46 Ibid., 490.

46 Ibid., 493.

48 Nehru, 44.

48 Ibid., 43.

50 Ibid., 44.

51 Gandhi, Autobiography, 456.

51 Ibid., 459–460.

54 William L. Shirer, Gandhi: A
Memoir, New York: Simon &
Schuster, 1979, page 34.

54 Patrick French, "History: The
Butcher of Amritsar, by Nigel
Collett," The Sunday (London)
Times, April 24, 2005, http://
entertainment.timesonline.co
.uk/tol/arts_and_entertainment/
books/article383052.ece
(March 5, 2008).

54 Gandhi, Autobiography, 471.

54 Nehru, 50.

55 Ibid., 69.

56 Catherine Fennelly, Textiles in
New England, 1790–1840 (Old
Sturbridge Village Booklet Series,
1961), Old Sturbridge, n.d.,
http://www.osv.org/explore
_learn/document_viewer
.php?Action=View&DocID=1066
(March 11, 2008).

56 Louis Fischer, Gandhi: His Life and
Message for the World (New York:
Penguin Books, [1962]), 72.

56 Nehru, 78.

57–58 Ibid., 79.

58–59 Mohandas Gandhi, "Statement
in the Great Trial," March 18,
1922, Wikisource, September
5, 2008, http://en.wikisource.
org/wiki/Statement_in_The
_Great_Trial (March 4, 2008).

59 New York Times, "Gandhi Seized
by British for Indefinite
Detention; Troops Posted for
Crisis," May 5, 1930, 1.

59 Fischer, 73.

60 Sarojini Naidu, letter from
Sarojini Naidu to Gandhiji,
July 20, 1926, n.d., http://
www.mkgandhi.org/
Selected%20Letters/Sarojini/
index.htm (January 5, 2010).

62 Nehru, 136–138.

62 Ibid., 137.

63 P. W. Wilson, "India Is Her
Own Worst Enemy," New York
Times, June 5, 1927, BR1.

63 New York Times, "Book by Miss
Mayo Rouses Hindu India,"
October 6, 1927, 6.

63 New York Times, "Gandhi Gives
View of Miss Mayo's Book,"
October 9, 1927, E3.

64 Sengupta, 209.

64 Ibid., 213.

64 Ibid.

64 Sarojini Naidu, letter to M. Gandhi, February 11, 1929, n.d., http://www.mkgandhi.org/Selected%20Letters/Sarojini/index.htm (March 11, 2008).

65 Sengupta., 221.

65 Ibid., 223.

66 Gene Sharp, *Gandhi Wields the Weapon of Moral Power* (Ahmadabad, India: Navajivan Publishing, 1960), 45.

66 *New York Times,* "India Nationalists Vote for Self-Rule," January 1, 1930, 7.

67 Sharp, 51.

67 Ibid., 53.

68 Upton Close, "Gandhi: The Prophet Who Sways India," *New York Times,* January 19, 1930, 77.

68 Sharp, 56.

68 Ibid., 57.

68 Weber, 84.

68 Sharp, 56.

69 *Time,* "March to the Sea," March 24, 1930, n.d., http://www.time.com/time/magazine/article/0,9171,738884-1,00.html (March 5, 2008).

69 Sailendra Nath Ghose, "Salt Used in Three Uprisings Prior to Gandhi Movement," *Washington Post,* May 18, 1930, M13.

69 C. F. Andrews, "Gandhi's Mystic Aims in His Indian March," *New York Times,* April 6, 1930, 144.

69 Sharp, 56.

70 Sharp, 66.

72 Weber, 117.

73 Ibid., 90.

74 Mahatma Gandhi Quotes, WorldofQuotes.com, 2006, http://www.worldofquotes.com/author/Mahatma-Gandhi/1/index.html (January 5, 2010).

75 Mohandas Gandhi, "On the Eve of the Dandi March Speech," March 11, 1930, September 5, 2008, http://en.wikisource.org/wiki/On_The_Eve_of_Dandi_March (March 5, 2008).

75 Ibid.

75 Ibid.

77 Weber, 137.

77–78 Ibid., 138.

78 Ibid., 141.

78 *Washington Post,* "Terrible Problem of India," March 13, 1930, 6.

79 Weber, 143.

81 Ibid., 159.

81 Weber, 160.

82 Nehru, 157.

82 Weber, 201.

83 Ibid., 206.

83 Ibid., 210.

84 Nehru, 159.

85 Weber, 271.

85 Ibid., 272.

85 Ibid., 273-274.

85 Ibid., 274.

86 Ibid., 288.

86 Sharp, 88.

86 Newton Phelps Stokes, II, "Marching with Gandhi," *Review of Reviews,* June 1930, 37.

86 Ibid., 38.

87 Weber, 317.

87 Associated Press, "Gandhi Makes Salt, Defying India's Law," *New York Times,* April 6, 1930, 1.

87 Weber, 326.

88 Mahatma Gandhi Quotes.

89 Weber, 333.

89 Ibid., 334.

89 Ibid., 335.

89 Ibid., 338.
90 Weber, 333.
91 Weber, 346.
91 Sharp, 89.
92 Weber, 346.
92 Ibid., 347.
92 *New York Times*, "Gandhi Asks
    Backing Here," April 7, 1930, 11.
93 Nehru, 160.
93 Ibid.
94 Sharp, 91.
95 Charles A. Selden, "England
    Approves Arrest of Gandhi,"
    New York Times, May 6, 1930, 6.
95 Nehru, 161.
95 Sharp, 106.
97 Weber, 402.
97 Ibid., 392.
97 Ibid., 393.
98 Sharp, 120-121.
98 Ibid.
98 Ibid.
98 Webb Miller, *I Found No Peace*
    (New York: The Literary
    Guild, 1936), 202.
99 *New York Times*, "Clergy Appeal
    to London," May 10, 1930, 10.
99–100 *New York Times*, "Labor Leader
    Scores M'Donald India Policy,"
    May 8, 1930, 10.
100 Weber, 477.
100 Miller, 192.
101 Shirer, 9.
101–102 Miller, 193.
102 Ibid., 195.
102 Nehru, 264.
102–103 Miller, 193.
103 Shirer, 99.
104 George Slocombe, "Gandhi
    Interviewed in Jail; Asks Full
    Freedom for India," *New York
    Times*, May 21, 1930, 1.
105 *New York Times*, "Boycott Hits
    Lancashire," May 8, 1930, 52.
106 *New York Times*, "Simon Report
    Urges Federation in India,
    Separating Burma," June 24,
    1930, 1.
106 *New York Times*, "Simon's Proposals
    Rejected," June 25, 1930, 11.
106 Ibid.
106 "Indian Conference," *Time*,
    November 24, 1930, n.d.,
    http://www.time
    .com/time/magazine/
    article/0,9171,740756,00.html
    (March 6, 2008).
106 Ibid.
107 Ibid.
108 Shirer, 41.
109 Sharp, 206.
109 Weber, 459.
109 Weber, 459.
110 Stanley Wolpert, *Nehru: A Tryst
    with Destiny* (New York: Oxford
    University Press: 1996), 126.
112 *Time*, "Landing Gandhi,"
    September 21, 1931, n.d.,
    http://www.time
    .com/time/magazine/
    article/0,9171,742272-2,00
    .html (March 6, 2008).
112 Ibid.
113 Nehru, 192.
117 Kasturba Memorial, 'Life
    Sketch of Kasturba," 2004,
    http://www.gandhi
    -manibhavan.org/kasturba/
    kasturba_lifesketch.htm
    (March 6, 2008).
119 Fischer, 175.
121 Mohandas Gandhi, "Speech at
    Prayer Meeting," January 16,
    1948, 2004, http://www
    .gandhi-manibhavan.org/
    gandhicomesalive/comesalive
    _originalvoice_16011948.htm
    (March 6, 2008).
121 Fischer, 189.
121 Ibid.

121 Jawaharlal Nehru, "The Light Has Gone Out," Speech on All India Radio, January 30, 1948, March 2, 2009, http://en.wikisource.org/wiki/The_Light_Has_Gone_Out (March 6, 2008).

123 G. H. Archambault, "Smuts Expresses Grief Over Gandhi," *New York Times*, January 31, 1948, 3.

123 *New York Times*, "Washington Feels Concern for India," January 31, 1948, 2.

123 Shirer, 227.

124 Mohandas Gandhi, quote by Anita Bora, "Echoes of the Mahatma," Rediff.com, October 2, 2002, http://www.rediff.com/search/2002/oct/02gandhi.htm (January 6, 2010).

125 Donald Szantho harrington, "John Hayes Holmes," n.d., http://members.fortunecity.com/hobeika/unitarians/holmes.html (March 7, 2008).

126 Taylor Branch, *Parting the Waters: America in the King Years, 1954-1963* (New York: Simon & Schuster, 1988), 171.

127 David J. Garrow, *Bearing the Cross: Martin Luther King, Jr. and the Southern Christian Leadership Conference* (New York: Vintage Books, 1988), 66.

128 John Haynes Holmes, *My Gandhi* (New York: Harper & Brothers, 1953), 22.

128 Ibid., 27

132 John Lewis with Michael D'Orso, *Walking with the Wind: A Memoir of the Movement* (San Diego: Harvest/Harcourt Brace, 1999), 169.

132 Branch, 609.

133–134 Lewis, 338.

134 Ibid.

134 Lewis, 344.

134 Gary G. Yerkey, "Hard Won Victory of Civil Rights Revisited," *Christian Science Monitor*, March 7, 2005, http://www.csmonitor.com/2005/0307/p03s01-ussc.html (March 7, 2008).

135 Martin Luther King, Jr., "Letter from a Birmingham Jail, April 16, 1963," Bates College, January 12, 2001, http://abacus.bates.edu/admin/offices/dos/mlk/letter.html (January 5, 2010).

136 American Experience website, *Citizen King*, January 19, 2004, http://www.pbs.org/wgbh/amex/mlk/sfeature/sf_bible.html (March 7, 2008)

136 Fischer, 8.

139 Mohandas Gandhi, "Gandhi's Quotations," 2004, http://www.gandhi-manibhavan.org/gandhicomesalive/n.htm#Non_Violence (March 7, 2008).

139 Lewis, 360.

139 Sharp, 88.

147 IndiaLife History.

SELECTED BIBLIOGRAPHY

Branch, Taylor. *Parting the Waters: America in the King Years, 1954-1963.* New York: Simon and Schuster, 1988.

Fischer, Louis. *Gandhi: His Life and Message for the World.* New York: Penguin Books, [1962].

Gandhi, Mohandas K. *An Autobiography: The Story of My Experiments with Truth.* Boston: Beacon Press, 1957.

Garrow, David J. *Bearing the Cross: Martin Luther King, Jr. and the Southern Christian Leadership Conference.* New York: Vintage Books, 1988.

James, Lawrence. *Raj: The Making and Unmaking of British India.* New York: St. Martin's Press, 1998.

Keay, John. *The Honourable Company: A History of the English East India Company.* New York: Macmillan, 1991.

————. *India: A History.* New York: Atlantic Monthly Press, 2000.

Kurlansky, Mark. *Salt: A World History.* New York: Penguin Books, 2003.

Lewis, John, with Michael D'Orso. *Walking with the Wind: A Memoir of the Movement.* San Diego: Harvest/Harcourt Brace, 1999.

Luce, Edward. *In Spite of the Gods: The Strange Rise of Modern India.* New York: Doubleday, 2007.

McNair, Sylvia. *India.* Chicago: Children's Press, 1990.

Miller, Webb. *I Found No Peace.* New York: The Literary Guild, 1936.

Moxham, Roy. *The Great Hedge of India.* New York: Carroll & Graf Publishers, 2001.

Nehru, Jawaharlal. *Toward Freedom: The Autobiography of Jawaharlal Nehru.* New York: The John Day Company, 1941.

Sengupta, Padmini. *Sarojini Naidu: A Biography.* New York: Asia Publishing House, 1966.

Sharp, Gene. *Gandhi Wields the Weapon of Moral Power.* Ahmadabad, India: Navajivan Publishing, 1960.

Shields, Charles J. *Mohandas K. Gandhi.* Philadelphia: Chelsea House, 2002.

Shirer, William L. *Gandhi: A Memoir.* New York: Simon & Schuster, 1979.

Thurman, Howard. *Jesus and the Disinherited.* Boston: Beacon Press, 1996.

Weber, Thomas. *On the Salt March: The Historiography of Gandhi's March to Dandi.* New Delhi, India: HarperCollins India, 1997.

Wolpert, Stanley. *Nehru: A Tryst with Destiny.* New York: Oxford University Press, 1996.

FURTHER READING, FILMS, AND WEBSITES

Books

Aronson, Marc. *The Real Revolution: The Global Story of American Independence.* New York: Clarion Books, 2005.

Engfer, Lee. *India in Pictures.* Minneapolis: Twenty-First Century Books, 2003.

Gandhi, Mohandas K. *An Autobiography: The Story of My Experiments with Truth.* Boston: Beacon Press, 1957.

Kurlansky, Mark. *Salt: A World History.* New York: Penguin Books, 2003.

Manheimer, Ann. *Martin Luther King Jr.* Minneapolis: Twenty-First Century Books, 2005.

Martin, Christopher. *Mohandas Gandhi.* Minneapolis: Twenty-First Century Books, 2001.

Taus-Bolstad, Stacy. *Pakistan in Pictures.* Minneapolis: Twenty-First Century Books, 2003.

Todd, Anne M. M. et al. *Mohandas Gandhi.* New York: Chelsea House Publishers, 2004.

Wilkinson, Philip. *Gandhi: The Young Protestor Who Founded a Nation.* Washington, DC: National Geographic Society, 2005.

Films

Gandhi. VHS & DVD. Directed and produced by Richard Attenborough. Los Angeles: Columbia Pictures, 1982.

The Jewel in the Crown. DVD. Directed by Christopher Moran. London: Granada Television, 1984.

Websites

The British Empire
http://www.britishempire.co.uk/
This website covers the vast history of the British Empire. Maps, biographies, timelines, and more help to sort out the complex story of the empire.

Congress of Racial Equality
http://www.core-online.org
This site explains how CORE was founded to apply Gandhian principles to end segregation in the United States. It also offers biographical information on CORE's leaders, including James Farmer and Bayard Rustin, and provides news about CORE in the twenty-first century.

Fellowship of Reconciliation
http://www.forusa.org/
The Fellowship of Reconciliation was instrumental in introducing Gandhian methods to the United States. The website discusses the group's history, focusing primarily on their present work for peace and justice.

A Force More Powerful
> http://www.aforcemorepowerful.org/films/index.php
> "A Force More Powerful" is a documentary series, aired on PBS in 2000, about the power of nonviolence to bring change. The website offers a wealth of stories and analysis about major nonviolent resistance movements, including the Salt March.

Gandhi in South Africa
> http://www.anc.org.za/ancdocs/history/people/gandhi/gandhisa.html
> This website, operated by the African National Congress, offers numerous articles, speeches, and more by Gandhi, concerning his work in South Africa.

GandhiServe Foundation: Mahatma Gandhi Research and Media Service
> http://www.gandhiserve.org
> GandhiServe features an impressive digital archive of Gandhi's articles and letters along with cartoons, video, and photographs.

Mani Bhavan Gandhi Information
> http://www.gandhi-manibhavan.org
> This comprehensive, well-organized website is notable, in particular, for its useful chronologies of Gandhi's life, broken down by era.

The Martin Luther King, Jr. Research and Education Institute
> http://www.stanford.edu/group/King/
> Stanford University in California houses Dr. King's papers and has developed an extensive website devoted to the U.S. civil rights movement. Check out the King Encyclopedia (from Home, select King Papers Project; then, under King resources, select King Encyclopedia).

MKGandhi.org
> http://www.mkgandhi.org/
> MKGandhi.org provides information on Gandhi's life, Gandhi-inspired organizations, museums and tourist sites, speeches, books, letters, and more. This site also provides an extensive archive of lively correspondence between Gandhi and Sarojini Naidu.

Seventy-Five Years of the Salt March: 1930–2005
> http://www.saltmarch.org.in/
> In 2005 people in cities worldwide commemorated Gandhi's Salt March with a Walk for Global Peace. This site celebrates the original march in 1930 with video clips, photographs, and information about the route, marchers, and more. It also provides details about the 2005 walk.

Trading Places: The East India Company and Asia, 1600–1834
> http://www.bl.uk/onlinegallery/features/trading/home.html
> This digital exhibition provides a lively explanation of how the East India Company became the dominant power in India and East Asia.

ABOUT THE AUTHOR

Betsy Kuhn's books for young readers include *The Race for Space: The United States and the Soviet Union Compete for the New Frontier*; *Prying Eyes: Privacy in the Twenty-first Century*; and *Angels of Mercy: The Army Nurses of World War II*. She lives in Maryland with her husband and twin sons.